Dedicated to

## *Beautiful Betty*

*~ 17th February 1947 - 29th July 2009 ~*

*...the joy in your heart,*
*...the smile on your face,*
*As you looked at this book*
*And took in each page;*
*So easy to imagine*
*If only you were here!*

*Why you had to go is still hard to understand,*
*But, I know our Father has a plan;*
*A plan that far transcends*
*...the thoughts of man*

*I miss you mum.*

# FACE to FACE

## ...A Closer Relationship

### akin olunloyo

SYNCTERFACE™

**SYNCTERFACE MEDIA**
**London, UK**
*www.syncterfacemedia.com*

# FACE TO FACE
*...A Closer Relationship*

ISBN: 978-0-9569741-0-5 - [Paperback]
ISBN: 978-1-9072942-8-0 - [Hardback ]
Copyright © July 2011 *akin olunloyo*
All Rights Reserved

Published in the United Kingdom by

SYNCTERFACE™

**Syncterface Media**
**London**
www.syncterfacemedia.com
info@syncterfacemedia.com

*Cover Design: Syncterface Media, London*
*Cover Photograph: Ella Pearl Photography*

This book is printed on acid-free paper

You hold in your hands a book that will challenge you to get to know your Heavenly Father and become all He has created you to be. Here is a call to leave your past behind and accept the divine invitation to come dine with Omnipotence; to come up higher to your place of face to face intimacy with God.

*"Face to Face... ...A Closer Relationship"*, beautifully shows how ordinary people who, in men's eyes, did not have much hope for greatness, came to experience supernatural success by virtue of their relationship with God. David the shepherd king, revealed his secret in the Psalms; "One thing have I desired of the Lord, that will I seek; that I may dwell in the house of the Lord all the days of my life, to gaze upon the beauty of the Lord and to seek Him in His temple". In Philippians, Paul, the onetime chief persecutor of the church said of the Lord, "that I may know Him and the power of His resurrection".

Akin writes to assure you that there is room for you too in His presence. What are you waiting for? The only thing you have to lose is your pain, guilt, misery and dissatisfaction with the mundane and ordinary.

Get ready for extraordinary living!"

*~ Rev. Inyang Okutinyang ~*
*Founding Pastor,*
*Foundation of Faith Fellowship, Sarnia, Ontario, Canada*
*Senior Pastor,*
*Christ Lovers Christian Centre, Lagos, Nigeria*

"An Exceptional book and a MUST READ for everyone who desires and seeks to live a victorious life in Christ Jesus. The principles in each chapter show that our God is still the same. It is the same principle of faith we need to walk in to please God and to live victoriously."

*~ Bayo & Funlola Akingbolagun ~*

"In this book Akin does a great job of reminding us of how much our Heavenly Father desires to have a deeper relationship with us. I love the way he shows by precepts and examples from the scriptures how this can be done. In a world that is now more concerned with the created than The Creator, this book is timely. This book in many ways is

A CALL TO TRUE WORSHIP."

*~ Adebayo Ademiju ~*
*Senior Pastor*
*Oasis of Love Christian Centre, London*

# APPRECIATION

### DEBS...
*My lady, My Snowflake, My darling wife; you are a constant and consistent source of inspiration, and your support and love for me are truly unending. I love you honey!*

### OYINDAMOLAOLUWA & OLUWATISHE...
*My Princesses, My precious daughters; you daily remind me of God's presence by the light and joy you bring into my life*

### AKIN & BUKOLA...
*True friends, they say, are hard to find so I guess I made the right choice by keeping mine. I daily thank God for bringing you guys into my life, and I know our Father will not forget your labour of love*

### KOREDE, BOSUN & YINKA...
*The Bible talks about a friend that sticks closer than a brother, but a friend that sticks closer than sibs like you I am yet to find. Thank you for being a constant source of encouragement*

### DAD...
*Those values you instilled in me, which I seemingly took for granted back in the day, have helped make me who I am today. Thank you so much dad!*

### PASTOR AGU IRUKWU AND PASTOR SOLA ADEAGA...
*For yielding to the Holy Spirit, and constantly ministering the pure, unadulterated Word of Truth into my life*

### PASTORS BAJO & CHIZOR AKISANYA...
*For taking out precious time to review this manuscript, and for writing a real, heartfelt foreword, thank you!*

### AND TO...
*Lady Ekezie, Olaitan, Lady Gibson-White, MoTru, Dreamy, Tolani and Minister J. Thanks for your probing, personal enthusiasm and prayers. Appreciate you lots!*

# CONTENTS

# FOREWORD

When asked to write this foreword I was both honoured and intrigued. Over the years I have had the privilege of watching *Akin* develop into an accomplished vocalist and song writer; he has in this capacity demonstrated a relationship with God that was obviously personal and genuine. The title of this book piqued my interest and my expectation increased with every passing chapter. I was in no way disappointed!

A personal relationship with God is the heart cry of God and man, yet for the latter it can be a source of intense disappointment and consternation. In this simple, heartfelt book, *Akin Olunloyo* has in many ways encapsulated what is the essence of a real relationship with God. He emphasises the fact that such a relationship is an attainable goal; for a kind God will not set a standard for us that is beyond our capabilities. *Akin* outlines the vast possibilities of a relationship with God in an easy-to-absorb conversational style of writing.

*Face to Face* is easy to read and can be read in parts or as a whole. It definitely presents itself to be a tome that will be returned to at different times in the reader's life. The ups and downs of a relationship with The Lord are depicted vividly through the lives of the variety of characters; thus ensuring that this book will be a valuable resource to a wide spectrum of readers, as well as speaking to the same reader time and time again, as both go through different phases of their journey, that is a vibrant relationship with their Heavenly Father.

It is my prayer that you have an enjoyable experience and are encouraged to develop a new lifestyle as you walk with and pursue God anew or afresh, but definitely *Face to Face.*

**Bajo Akisanya**
*Director of Youth*
*Jesus House for all Nations, London*

# PREFACE

It was the month of August in the year two thousand and eight and a work I had been involved in for about ten years was being "threatened" by a word from *my Employer*. When initially I was told that my time on the job was up a part of me said, "I don't think so". I proceeded to tell *my Employer* that I would let this work go if He would let me know what He wanted me to do next, but all I seemed to hear was *"Let go and let Me"*. Now, that simply was not good enough for me because *I needed to know*.

Weeks of silence followed and understandably, I began to feel a little uncomfortable. I mean, how would you feel if The One who gives you the ability to do the work you do suddenly came and said He wanted you off the job? I found a bit of comfort in constantly telling myself that I was waiting for a response; after all, *I needed to know* what He wanted me to do next. Until then I intended to keep my hands on the plough and stay put.

Somehow I knew I was really pushing it because the work

became more of a struggle. I still enjoyed it but my power and might was now playing a bigger role and, knowing the way *my Employer* operates, that was not a good sign.

Anyway, those who know The One I work for will understand when I say, *"He is full of mercy"*, and it was out of His tender mercy that He chose to lead me to the Book of Genesis chapter 12:1-3. These were verses I had read a number of times; verses that, until now, had never really been personal to me:

> *¹Now the LORD had said unto Abram, Get thee out of thy country, and from thy kindred, and from thy father's house, UNTO A LAND THAT I WILL SHEW THEE:*
> *²And I will make of thee a great nation, and I will bless thee, and make thy name great; and thou shalt be a blessing:*
> *³And I will bless them that bless thee, and curse him that curseth thee: and in thee shall all families of the earth be blessed.*

*Genesis 12:1-3*

*{Being honest, it was only verse 1 that initially caught my attention but verses 2 & 3 were a bonus I was willing to accept!}*

So, the message was now clear *{I guess it always was but until now I had stubbornly resisted}*: **The time had come for me to move out of my "comfort zone" to a place I had no clue about.** The message on "CHANGE" had been coming from the pulpit for months; was this it for me?

---

*As I dug into God's word it dawned on me afresh that our Father has always had one heartfelt desire...*

---

Once I accepted the word from *my Employer*, who by now I believe you know, I started getting this feeling that it was time to take my relationship with Him to, not just another level, but a deeper level. God was telling me that it was time to stop thinking outside the box and get rid of the box altogether, because the box would always be an object of limitation.

This simultaneously threw me into a state of anxiety and excitement. I thought I had touched down when I saw the light on *"thinking outside the box"* but here was God telling me to get rid of the old faithful box, and the limitations that came with it, and to truly see Him as the Limitless One.

So, with my heart alight, my adventure began. A deep desire to know more about The Father took me back to the very beginning; the book of Genesis! As I dug into God's word it dawned on me afresh that our Father has always had one heartfelt desire: t*o have an intimate, face to face relationship with His ultimate creation: MANKIND!*

Through this book I would like to invite you on a brief journey; a journey into the lives of Adam, Abraham, Isaac, Jacob, Moses, David and the Son of man Himself, Jesus Christ. As we peep into their lives we will see what made them so special in God's eyes, and what made their relationship with God so real and personal. This I believe will help us understand the depth and intimacy our Father desires in the relationship He shares with us, His children.

I pray that as you peruse and ponder with an open heart, the words of this book will be of eternal value, taking your relationship with The Father to mind blowing, limitless heights. So, sit tight and enjoy the ride.

# God's Ultimate Creation

First let us take a look at Adam. From the very beginning of time there was always something special about man. For five days God spent time putting the world together and at the end of each day He stepped back, took a look at the work of His hands and saw that it was good. Then came the sixth day!

---

*Creation was not complete until God created man*

---

## The sixth day

In Genesis chapter 1 we see that God started the sixth day by creating the cattle, *"the creepies"*, and the beast of the earth. When this was done God once again took a look and He *saw that it was good*. Prior to this, God only declared the works of His hands as good after He had finished His work for the day. So what made the sixth day so different?

> [24] *And God said, Let the earth bring forth the living creature after his kind, cattle, and creeping thing, and beast of the earth after his kind: and it was so.*

Creation was not complete until God created man, and it was only after God had completed creation that He stepped back, smiled and *saw that it was very good*. Could one therefore conclude that it was only after the creation of man that God Himself upgraded the status of His creation from *"good"* to *"very good"*? I believe God had saved the very best for last. *Mankind was the icing on the cake; he was God's ultimate creation!*

## God's ultimate creation

It goes without saying that mankind was special. Made in the image and likeness of God and given dominion over everything that God had created, it seems quite clear that God made mankind to be His replica on earth.

*HAVE DOMINION OVER THE FISH OF THE SEA, AND OVER THE FOWL OF THE AIR, AND OVER EVERY LIVING THING THAT MOVETH UPON THE EARTH.*

*[29] And God said, Behold, I have given you every herb bearing seed, which is upon the face of all the earth, and every tree, in the which is the fruit of a tree yielding seed; to you it shall be for meat.*

*[30] And to every beast of the earth, and to every fowl of the air, and to every thing that creepeth upon the earth, wherein there is life, I have given every green herb for meat: and it was so.*

*Genesis 1:26-30*

Reading through these verses I can almost hear God saying, *"I have made you just like Me. Over all My creation you have authority. So take good care of it, be fruitful and multiply; to you I entrust this creation of Mine"*.

*[8] And the LORD God planted a garden eastward in Eden; and there he put the man whom he had formed.*

*[9] And out of the ground made the LORD God to grow every tree that is pleasant to the sight, and good for food; the tree of life also in the midst of the garden, and the tree of knowledge of good and evil.*

*[15] And the LORD God took the man, and put him into the garden of Eden to dress it and to keep it.*

*Genesis 2:8-9, 15*

---

## *Adam was able to connect to the mind of God because of the relationship he had with God*

---

God's original intent after creating the earth was to grant mankind dominion, sovereign authority over all His creation, just like He has sovereign authority. So, when God planted the Garden in Eden, a garden that lacked no good thing, and placed Adam in it the plan was set in motion.

## Divine relationship

Adam did not lack a thing but the satisfaction he derived from living a *"lack-free"* life was nothing compared to the fulfilment that originated from him knowing God. Adam shared a bond with God that anyone would *envy*. Adam had intimate fellowship with God.

> [19] *And out of the ground the LORD God formed every beast of the field, and every fowl of the air; and brought them unto Adam to see what he would call them: AND WHATSOEVER ADAM CALLED EVERY LIVING CREATURE, THAT WAS THE NAME THEREOF.*
> [20] *AND ADAM GAVE NAMES TO ALL CATTLE, AND TO THE FOWL OF THE AIR, AND TO EVERY BEAST OF THE FIELD; but for Adam there was not found an help meet for him.*
>
> *Genesis 2:19-20*

The relationship God had with Adam was perfect. The intimacy shared in their relationship is seen when, after forming every living creature, God brought each creature to Adam for a name. We recall from *verse 19* of Genesis chapter 2 that *"...whatsoever Adam called every living creature that was the name thereof"*. Knowing that God knew the name of every creature before He even created them implies that when God brought each creature to Adam, Adam named each animal what God had already called them in the realm of the spirit. Adam was only able to do this because he was connected to the mind of God. Adam was able to connect to the mind of God because of the relationship he had with God!

> [8] *AND THEY HEARD THE VOICE OF THE LORD GOD WALKING IN THE GARDEN IN THE COOL OF THE DAY: and Adam and his wife hid themselves from the presence of the LORD God amongst the trees of the garden.*
> [9] *And the LORD God called unto Adam, and said unto him, WHERE ART THOU?*
>
> *Genesis 3:8-9*

That Adam and Eve were *hiding* from God's presence signified that they were doing something they did not do normally. Their hiding implied that there was something wrong with their divine relationship. God calling Adam and saying *"Where art thou?"* had nothing to do with God being confused about his whereabouts. It had everything to do with the relationship that God shared with Adam. **Man naturally lived his life before God; MAN LIVED IN GOD'S PRESENCE.** *{Hiding from the One he shared a personal relationship with was purely a result of unfaithfulness}.*

Another interesting thing to note is that, God walking in the garden in the cool of the day was not a one-off occurrence. Adam and Eve KNEW God's voice because they regularly fellowshipped with Him.

> [2] *But he that entereth in by the door is the shepherd of the sheep.*
> [3] *To him the porter openeth; and the sheep hear his voice: and he calleth his own sheep by name, and leadeth them out.*
> [4] *And when he putteth forth his own sheep, he goeth before them, and the sheep follow him: for they know his voice.*
>
> *John 10:2-4*

---

### God created man to dwell in His presence

---

The sheep know the voice of the shepherd because he is the one that constantly takes them out to feed on green pastures and drink from the still waters; the sheep know the voice of the shepherd because they spend time with the shepherd. *The only way to get familiar with someone's voice is by spending time with that someone.*

**Man knew the voice of God because he spent time with God.** Adam and Eve spent time in God's presence.

The more time they spent with God the more they knew the mind of God, and the more they actually *"became"* like God. *But, I thought man was made in God's image and after God's likeness anyway?* Well, he was but he needed to spend time in the presence of The Creator for him to become whom he was created to be.

The perfect example is when you decided to place your life in Jesus' hands. The second you received Christ into your heart you became a new creation; you became *"more than a conqueror"*; you became the righteousness of God in Christ. However, you did not start walking in the fullness of this new nature simply because you did not have a full understanding of who you had become. As you spend time in the presence of the word of God, with the help of the Holy Spirit, the reality of the new nature sets in and you gradually become who you already are.

Unfortunately, man's time in God's presence came to an abrupt end when Eve was deceived, Adam was persuaded, and they both disobeyed God's first commandment given in Genesis chapter 2:16-17. However, here we clearly see God's blueprint when it comes to His relationship with mankind. *God created man to dwell in His presence. As they fellowshipped together man would grow to know the voice and mind of God, and as man listened to and obeyed God's voice he would become who God predestined him to be.*

# FATHER OF THE FAITHFUL

Then there was Father Abraham. Abraham is commonly known as Father of the faithful but have you ever sat back and asked, "Why?" Though Abraham walked in faith he was not the first person to go on a faith walk with God. The scriptures record that Enoch walked with God and his life pleased God so much that God did not let him die. God simply whisked him away:

> *24 And Enoch walked with God: and he was not; for God took him.*
>
> *Genesis 5:24*

Then there was Noah. He was a just and perfect man in his time, and he also walked with God:

> *9 These are the generations of Noah: Noah was a just man and perfect in his generations, and Noah walked with God.*
>
> *Genesis 6:9*

So, how come Abraham is called the father of the faithful and not Enoch, or even Noah?

# Chosen by God

From the scriptures we see that Noah and Abraham share a number of similarities:

## 1. Noah was a man of faith...

*[7]BY FAITH NOAH, being warned of God of things not seen as yet, moved with fear, prepared an ark to the saving of his house; by the which he condemned the world, and became heir of the righteousness which is by faith.*

*Hebrews 11:7*

## ...Abraham was a man of faith

*[8]BY FAITH ABRAHAM, when he was called to go out into a place which he should after receive for an inheritance, obeyed; and he went out, not knowing whither he went.*

*Hebrews 11:8*

## 2. God established a covenant with Noah...

*[11]AND I WILL ESTABLISH MY COVENANT WITH YOU, neither shall all flesh be cut off any more by the waters of a flood; neither shall there any more be a flood to destroy the earth. [12]And God said, This is the token of the covenant which I make between me and you and every living creature that is with you, for perpetual generations: [13]I do set my bow in the cloud, and it shall be for a token of a covenant between me and the earth. [17]AND GOD SAID UNTO NOAH, This is the token of the covenant, which I have established between me and all flesh that is upon the earth.*

*Genesis 9:11-13, 17*

## ...God established a covenant with Abraham

*[7]AND I WILL ESTABLISH MY COVENANT BETWEEN ME AND THEE and thy seed after thee in their generations for an everlasting covenant, to be a God unto thee, and to thy seed after thee. [8]And I will give unto thee, and to thy seed after thee, the land wherein thou art a stranger, all the land of Canaan, for an everlasting possession; and I will be their God. [9]AND GOD SAID UNTO ABRAHAM, Thou shalt keep my*

*covenant therefore, thou, and thy seed after thee in their generations.*

*Genesis 17:7-9*

### 3. Noah worshipped The Almighty God...

[20]*And NOAH BUILDED AN ALTAR UNTO THE LORD; and took of every clean beast, and of every clean fowl, and offered burnt offerings on the altar.*

[21]*And the LORD smelled a sweet savour; and the LORD said in his heart, I will not again curse the ground any more for man's sake; for the imagination of man's heart is evil from his youth; neither will I again smite any more every thing living, as I have done.*

*Genesis 8:20-21*

### ...Abraham worshipped The Almighty God

[7]*And the LORD appeared unto Abram, and said, Unto thy seed will I give this land: and there builded he an altar unto the LORD, who appeared unto him.*

[8]*And he removed from thence unto a mountain on the east of Bethel, and pitched his tent, having Bethel on the west, and Hai on the east: and there he builded an altar unto the LORD, and called upon the name of the LORD.*

*Genesis 12:7-8*

However, unlike Noah, the scriptures do not describe Abraham as a *perfect* man. Abraham was raised in a city called Ur in Chaldea. It was an idolatrous city that worshiped pagan gods. Terah, Abraham's father, then left Ur, with Abraham, and the rest of the clan, and finally arrived at a place called Haran. This was where Terah re-established his household:

[31]*And Terah took Abram his son, and Lot the son of Haran his son's son, and Sarai his daughter in law, his son Abram's wife; and they went forth with them from Ur of the Chaldees, to go into the land of Canaan; and they came unto Haran, and dwelt there.*

*Genesis 11:31*

This would not have helped Abraham that much because

his father was an idol worshipper. Therefore in Haran, under his father's dominion, Abram still lived in an idolatrous environment.

> <sup>2</sup>And Joshua said unto all the people, Thus saith the LORD God of Israel, Your fathers dwelt on the other side of the flood in old time, even Terah, the father of Abraham, and the father of Nachor: and they served other gods.
>
> Joshua 24:2

But, despite Abraham's imperfect background God still chose him. This goes to show that truly *it is not of him that willeth, nor of him that runneth, but of God that sheweth mercy.* At times I sit back and wonder why God chose someone like Abraham to be the father of the faithful and the more I ponder the more I understand why. *When God picks you up from the dumps and makes you a delight in His sight your self-righteousness turns to ashes. You become completely empty and He fills you up with Himself!* Anyway, back to Abraham.

---

*God called Abraham out of a place of idol worship so He could bring him into a place of Godly worship*

---

It is quite fascinating that in the midst of these *"unfavourable"* conditions Abraham still managed to hear God's voice, believe God's word and, by faith, follow God's instruction. Let us take a look at Genesis chapter 12:

> <sup>1</sup>Now the LORD had said unto Abram, Get thee out of thy country, and from thy kindred, and from thy father's house, unto a land that I will shew thee:
> <sup>2</sup>And I will make of thee a great nation, and I will bless thee, and make thy name great; and thou shalt be a blessing:
> <sup>3</sup>And I will bless them that bless thee, and curse him that curseth thee: and in thee shall all families of the earth be blessed.
> <sup>4</sup>So Abram departed, as the LORD had spoken unto him; and

*Lot went with him: and Abram was seventy and five years old when he departed out of Haran.*
⁵*And Abram took Sarai his wife, and Lot his brother's son, and all their substance that they had gathered, and the souls that they had gotten in Haran; and they went forth to go into the land of Canaan; and into the land of Canaan they came.*

*Genesis 12:1-5*

God told Abraham to leave his country, his relatives and, his father's house. **This was a call of Separation.** God called Abraham out of a place of *idol worship* so He could bring him into a place of *Godly worship.* It was important for Abram to leave his father's dominion, which embraced the worship of pagan gods, and establish his own household where he would have dominion; *a household that would embrace the worship of The Almighty God.* As Abraham stepped out in faith he would grow to know God as **El Shaddai** *{the All Sufficient God; the All Powerful God that overpowers all powers},* and become who God had predestined him to be.

As Abraham obeyed the call he became the recipient of God's seven fold promise:

i.    A promise *to make Abraham a great nation.* A nation that would have both **quantity of people** *{hence the reason for the name change from Abram, "exalted father", to Abraham, "father of a multitude"}* and **quality of character** *{a holy people, according to God's holiness}.* This was a promise to make Abraham and his descendants God's own people

ii.   A promise to *bless Abraham* as an individual

iii.  A promise to *make Abraham's name great*

iv.   A promise that Abraham himself will be *a blessing* to others

v.   A promise *to bless those who bless* Abraham and his seed

vi.  A promise to *curse "**him**" who curses* Abraham and his seed.

vii. Finally, God promised that *in thee, Abraham, shall ALL families of the earth be blessed.* This promise is reiterated in Genesis chapter 22:

> <sup>15</sup>*And the angel of the LORD called unto Abraham out of heaven the second time,*
> <sup>16</sup>*And said, By myself have I sworn, saith the LORD, for because thou hast done this thing, and hast not withheld thy son, thine only son:*
> <sup>17</sup>*That in blessing I will bless thee, and in multiplying I will multiply thy seed as the stars of the heaven, and as the sand which is upon the sea shore; and thy seed shall possess the gate of his enemies;*
> <sup>18</sup>*And in thy seed shall all the nations of the earth be blessed; because thou hast obeyed my voice.*
>
> *Genesis 22:15-18*

The phrase *"in thy seed"* refers to the seed of the woman mentioned in Genesis chapter 3; the Messiah, the promised deliverer who would crush the serpent's head. *Jesus was the seed of Abraham:*

> <sup>15</sup>*And I will put enmity between thee and the woman, and between thy seed and her seed; it shall bruise thy head, and thou shalt bruise his heel.*
>
> *Genesis 3:15*
>
> <sup>16</sup>*Now to Abraham and his seed were the promises made. He saith not, And to seeds, as of many; but as of one, AND TO THY SEED, WHICH IS CHRIST.*
>
> *Galatians 3:16*

---

### God's redemption plan for all mankind is revealed in the promise that He made to Abraham.

---

It goes without saying that the coming of Jesus Christ revolutionized the world. Today, the good news is being preached in every nation and salvation is freely offered to everyone. All over the world men have heard the Gospel and by faith have received salvation through Jesus Christ. The devil tried to break God's promise but all his efforts were in vain. *God's redemption plan for all mankind is revealed in the promise that He made to Abraham.* This promise will stand until God's plan comes to pass.

It now becomes easy to understand why Abraham is called the father of the faithful. Because of *Abraham's seed* multitudes in all the nations of the earth have come to believe and have faith in the One True and Living God.

## Walk before Me

In the book of Genesis chapter 17 God specifically commands Abram to *"walk before Me, and be thou perfect"*:

> [1]*And when Abram was ninety years old and nine, the LORD appeared to Abram, and said unto him, I am the Almighty God; walk before me, and be thou perfect.*
>
> *Genesis 17:1*

From here onwards Abraham walked *before* God {*Genesis 24:40 and Genesis 48:15*}. However, prior to this the Bible records that both Enoch and Noah walked *with* God. One could easily say that this is purely a play of words, but somehow I do not think so. Even though walking *"with"* God and walking *"before"* God both point to having a relationship with God, I believe God was telling Abram that it was time to take their relationship to another level.

The actual Hebrew word behind the phrase *"before Me"* in Genesis chapter 17:1 turns out to be *"paw-neem"*, which literally is the plural form of the word *"face"*. Also, the Hebrew word translated as *"perfect"* in the same verse is

*"Taw-meem"*, which actually means *expended, exhausted, depleted, spent, completely empty or to come to an end,* as in *"come to the end of oneself".*

A more literal translation of the latter part of Genesis chapter 17:1 could then read:

*"...; walk before My faces, and be completely empty of yourself."*

Suddenly, God's relationship with Abram takes on a whole new dimension. Up till now Abram would have known God as Elohim *{the Creator of all things},* El Elyon *{the Most High God},* and Adonai *{my Lord, my Master}* but here God shows another face. He appears to Abram as El-Shaddai *{the Many Breasted, All Sufficient One}.* This awesome experience brings Abram to his knees. Abram falls on his face and by the time he arises God had changed his name.

---

*...the more Abraham "emptied" himself, the more God filled him up with Himself*

---

Here was God telling Abram to completely empty himself and walk in the presence of The One who is able to do all things. As Abraham obeyed he would experience the manifestation of God's many sides, God's many faces. A picture of God's grace then begins to shine through as it becomes apparent that unmerited favour would accompany Abraham throughout his lifetime.

Even though Abraham had a few *"doubt blips"*, such as the *"Ishmael issue"*, as he lived his life in the presence of the All Sufficient One, with his trust focussed solely on Him, Abraham began to experience mind blowing depths of

God. An example of the depth of relationship Abraham shared with The Almighty God is recorded in Genesis chapter 18:

> [17] *And the LORD said, Shall I hide from Abraham that thing which I do;*
> [18] *Seeing that Abraham shall surely become a great and mighty nation, and all the nations of the earth shall be blessed in him?*
> [19] *For I know him, that he will command his children and his household after him, and they shall keep the way of the LORD, to do justice and judgment; that the LORD may bring upon Abraham that which he hath spoken of him.*
>
> *Genesis 18:17-19*

Here God was about to destroy the lands of Sodom and Gomorrah because of their grievous sin. However, He had a bit of a situation; "*...Shall I hide from Abraham that thing which I do;*" It almost sounds like God is *tempted* not to let Abraham in on His Sodom and Gomorrah plan, but because of the covenant relationship they shared, and out of His tender mercy, He dropped a hint.

I guess a reason why God may have considered not telling Abraham about Sodom and Gomorrah was because He knew Abraham. I also believe it was because **GOD KNEW THAT ABRAHAM KNEW HIM.** Remember, Abraham was living his life in the presence of God; *the more Abraham "emptied" himself, the more God filled him up with Himself.*

> [20] *And the LORD said, Because the cry of Sodom and Gomorrah is great, and because their sin is very grievous;*
> [21] *I will go down now, and see whether they have done altogether according to the cry of it, which is come unto me; and if not, I will know.*
> [22] *And the men turned their faces from thence, and went toward Sodom: but Abraham stood yet before the LORD.*
> [23] *And Abraham drew near, and said, Wilt thou also destroy*

*the righteous with the wicked?*

*²⁴Peradventure there be fifty righteous within the city: wilt thou also destroy and not spare the place for the fifty righteous that are therein?*

*²⁵That be far from thee to do after this manner, to slay the righteous with the wicked: and that the righteous should be as the wicked, that be far from thee: Shall not the Judge of all the earth do right?*

*²⁶And the LORD said, If I find in Sodom fifty righteous within the city, then I will spare all the place for their sakes.*

*²⁷And Abraham answered and said, Behold now, I have taken upon me to speak unto the LORD, which am but dust and ashes:*

*²⁸Peradventure there shall lack five of the fifty righteous: wilt thou destroy all the city for lack of five? And he said, If I find there forty and five, I will not destroy it.*

*²⁹And he spake unto him yet again, and said, Peradventure there shall be forty found there. And he said, I will not do it for forty's sake.*

*³⁰And he said unto him, Oh let not the LORD be angry, and I will speak: Peradventure there shall thirty be found there. And he said, I will not do it, if I find thirty there.*

*³¹And he said, Behold now, I have taken upon me to speak unto the LORD: Peradventure there shall be twenty found there. And he said, I will not destroy it for twenty's sake.*

*³²And he said, Oh let not the LORD be angry, and I will speak yet but this once: Peradventure ten shall be found there. And he said, I will not destroy it for ten's sake.*

*³³And the LORD went his way, as soon as he had left communing with Abraham: and Abraham returned unto his place.*

*Genesis 18:20-33*

Taking a closer look at these verses we see that God did not actually let Abraham in on the totality of His Sodom and Gomorrah plan. God simply told Abraham that He would be going down to check things out *{verses 20-21}*. But Abraham knew God; **ABRAHAM KNEW THE MIND OF GOD.**

*³For what saith the scripture? Abraham believed God, and it*

*was counted unto him for righteousness.*
⁴*Now to him that worketh is the reward not reckoned of grace, but of debt.*
⁵*But to him that worketh not, but believeth on him that justifieth the ungodly, his faith is counted for righteousness.*

Romans 4:3-5

⁶*For when we were yet without strength, in due time Christ died for the ungodly.*
¹⁰*For if, when we were enemies, we were reconciled to God by the death of his Son, much more, being reconciled, we shall be saved by his life.*

Romans 5:6, 10

By faith, Abraham believed that God was able to justify the ungodly. *{In the Old Testament I believe this is the closest any man came to understanding the justification that would be made available to the ungodly through the death of Christ}.* Hence by asking God over and over again if He would destroy the city if there were 50, 45, 40, 30, 20 or 10 righteous people in the land Abraham was also standing in the gap for the ungodly. Abraham knew that if God would not *slay the righteous with the wicked,* in saving the righteous the ungodly would also be spared. Unfortunately, ten righteous people did not exist in the land and that was the end of Sodom and Gomorrah.

We should also remember Abram's name change. When God changed Abram's name to Abraham, declaring him to be *"a father of nations"*, God also changed Abraham's heart. *With a change of name came a change of heart;* Abraham now had a father's heart *{he was beginning to take on the very nature of God}.* I personally believe that, even though Abraham believed that God was able to justify the ungodly, he also felt a sense of responsibility for these two cities hence the reason why he naturally stood in the gap. *A father's heart!*

God's relationship with Abraham is simply amazing. Abraham exposed himself to God yet did not feel insecure. Abraham willingly surrendered his joys and fears to God knowing he was safe because he was also being watched over by God. Abraham's life was like an open book before God; he told God everything about himself as if God knew nothing about him, yet knowing that The Most High God knew everything about him.

So, Abraham, *the completely empty and totally dependent one*, walked in the many faces of The Almighty God; *the Completely Full and All Sufficient One*. Abraham lived a life totally reliant on The One who was able to do all things; he emptied himself so that God could fill him up with Himself. Abraham lived his life in the very presence of God; *no wonder God called Abraham His friend.*

> [8] *But thou, Israel, art my servant, Jacob whom I have chosen,* **THE SEED OF ABRAHAM MY FRIEND.**
>
> *Isaiah 41:8*
>
> [23] *And the scripture was fulfilled which saith, Abraham believed God, and it was imputed unto him for righteousness:* **AND HE WAS CALLED THE FRIEND OF GOD.**
>
> *James 2:23*

# CHILD OF PROMISE

In steps Isaac. From the scriptures we understand that God was not only the God of Abraham, He was also the God of Isaac. This leads me to believe that there was something peculiar about Isaac.

> [15]And God said moreover unto Moses, Thus shalt thou say unto the children of Israel, the LORD God of your fathers, the God of Abraham, THE GOD OF ISAAC, and the God of Jacob, hath sent me unto you: this is my name for ever, and this is my memorial unto all generations.
>
> Exodus 3:15

## ...the word became flesh

Isaac's birth had nothing to do with Abraham's body or Sarah's womb because the scriptures clearly state that these were "dead" {Romans 4:19}. Isaac was the physical manifestation of a divine promise; a word from God. It was this word from God that gave life to Sarah's dead womb thus making Sarah fruitful in her old age. This promise made to Abraham concerning Isaac's birth was the word that God spoke to Abraham in Genesis chapter 17:

> [19]AND GOD SAID, SARAH THY WIFE SHALL BEAR THEE A

*SON INDEED; and thou shalt call his name Isaac: and I will establish my covenant with him for an everlasting covenant, and with his seed after him.*

*Genesis 17:19*

Isaac was a child of promise {*Galatians 4:22-23, 28*}; the fulfilment of God's promise to Abraham. His birth was not after the flesh but according to a word from God, similar to the birth of JESUS:

*[18]Now the birth of Jesus Christ was on this wise: When as his mother Mary was espoused to Joseph, before they came together, she was found with child of the Holy Ghost.*

*[19]Then Joseph her husband, being a just man, and not willing to make her a public example, was minded to put her away privily.*

*[20]But while he thought on these things, behold, the angel of the LORD appeared unto him in a dream, saying, Joseph, thou son of David, fear not to take unto thee Mary thy wife: for that which is conceived in her is of the Holy Ghost.*

*Matthew 1:18-20*

Suddenly a number of similarities between Isaac and Jesus seem to jump out:

**1.   God told Abraham to sacrifice his ONLY SON, ISAAC** {*the "Ishmael question" could pop up here but remember ISAAC WAS THE ONLY PROMISED CHILD OF ABRAHAM. It is also interesting to note that Ishmael was born to Abram while Isaac was born to Abraham*};

*[2]And he said, TAKE NOW THY SON, THINE ONLY SON ISAAC, whom thou lovest, and get thee into the land of Moriah; and offer him there for a burnt offering upon one of the mountains which I will tell thee of.*

*Genesis 22:2*

*...God gave His ONLY SON, JESUS;*

*[16]For God so loved the world, that he gave HIS ONLY*

BEGOTTEN SON, that whosoever believeth in him should not perish, but have everlasting life.

John 3:16

## 2. Isaac carried the wood on which he was to be sacrificed;

*6And Abraham TOOK THE WOOD OF THE BURNT OFFERING, AND LAID IT UPON ISAAC HIS SON; and he took the fire in his hand, and a knife; and they went both of them together.*

Genesis 22:6

### ...Jesus carried the cross on which he was crucified;

*17And he bearing his cross went forth into a place called the place of a skull, which is called in the Hebrew Golgotha;*

John 19:17

## 3. Isaac was to be sacrificed on a mountain in the land of Moriah;

*2And he said, Take now thy son, thine only son Isaac, whom thou lovest, AND GET THEE INTO THE LAND OF MORIAH; AND OFFER HIM THERE FOR A BURNT OFFERING UPON ONE OF THE MOUNTAINS WHICH I WILL TELL THEE OF.*

Genesis 22:2

### ...Jesus was crucified in Golgotha in the land of Moriah;

*17And he bearing his cross went forth into a place called the place of a skull, WHICH IS CALLED IN THE HEBREW GOLGOTHA:*
*18WHERE THEY CRUCIFIED HIM, and two other with him, on either side one, and Jesus in the midst.*

John 19:17-18

*{Golgotha is said to be located on a saddle point on a mount in the land of Moriah. It is also said to be the same mount on which Isaac was offered as a sacrifice!}*

### 4.  Abraham gave his son all he had;

> [5]*And Abraham gave all that he had unto Isaac.*
>
> *Genesis 25:5*

### ...God made His Son the Heir of all things;

> [2]*Hath in these last days spoken unto us by HIS SON, WHOM HE HATH APPOINTED HEIR OF ALL THINGS, by whom also he made the worlds;*
>
> *Hebrews 1:2*

Even Isaac's three-day journey to the mountains in the land of Moriah may well be linked to the three days Jesus spent in the grave.

For a second, can you imagine the thoughts that must have flashed through Abraham's mind as they set out for Moriah? How he had to consider Isaac dead, and trust totally in God to somehow bring his promised child back to life so as fulfil His promise? Not easy, but I guess that is what this faith walk is all about!

There are a number of similarities that suggest that Isaac was *a type of Christ.* However, one which I believe to be so profound is that, just like He did with Jesus, God named Isaac from his mother's womb:

### ...call his name Isaac;

> [19]*And God said, Sarah thy wife shall bear thee a son indeed; AND THOU SHALT CALL HIS NAME ISAAC: and I will establish my covenant with him for an everlasting covenant, and with his seed after him.*
>
> *Genesis 17:19*

### ...call His name Jesus;

> [21]*And she shall bring forth a son, AND THOU SHALT CALL*

*HIS NAME JESUS: for he shall save his people from their sins.*

*Matthew 1:21*

*{In the scriptures there was no one named, or renamed, by God who did not have a divine purpose}*

## The faith test

Unlike his father, who accomplished things that had never been done before, Isaac really did not do anything new; *at least that is what we are made to believe.* Isaac experienced nothing new and in a sense, one could say all Isaac did was eat the fruit of his father's labour.

> ²*And the LORD appeared unto him, and said, Go not down into Egypt; dwell in the land which I shall tell thee of:*
> ³*Sojourn in this land, and I will be with thee, and will bless thee; for unto thee, and unto thy seed, I will give all these countries, and I will perform the oath which I sware unto Abraham thy father;*
> ⁴*And I will make thy seed to multiply as the stars of heaven, and will give unto thy seed all these countries; and in thy seed shall all the nations of the earth be blessed;*
> ⁵*BECAUSE THAT ABRAHAM OBEYED MY VOICE, AND KEPT MY CHARGE, MY COMMANDMENTS, MY STATUTES, AND MY LAWS.*
> ²⁴*And the LORD appeared unto him the same night, and said, I am the God of Abraham thy father: fear not, for I am with thee, and will bless thee, and multiply thy seed FOR MY SERVANT ABRAHAM'S SAKE.*

*Genesis 26:2-5, 24*

These verses of scripture seem to shed more light on the fact that the relationship God had with Isaac was actually based on the bond He had with Abraham. So, the question is, "*did God really share anything special with Isaac?*"

One thing we sometimes fail to realise is that Isaac was not exactly a little child when his father wanted to offer him up as a burnt offering on a mount in the land of

Moriah. Let me explain.

---

*...not once do we see Isaac try to out run or overpower his father, something I believe he could have done with relative ease.*

---

Isaac's age at this time is not exactly clear from scripture but two things about him stand out. First of all we realise that Isaac had to walk the three day journey as the only donkey available carried his elderly father, and the wood for the burnt offering {*Genesis 22:3*}. Secondly, we see that Isaac actually had to carry the wood, probably on his back, up the mountain to where his father would set up the altar {*Genesis 22:6*}. These imply that most likely Isaac was no longer a little boy and point to the possibility that he was, at least, approaching manhood.

As Abraham and his son walked up the mountain Isaac could not help but ask, "*...Behold the fire and the wood: but where is the lamb for a burnt offering?*" If Isaac had not caught on to what was about to happen to him here, reality soon dawned when he and his father arrived at the place where God had told Abraham to offer the burnt offering:

> *⁹And they came to the place which God had told him of; and Abraham built an altar there, and laid the wood in order, and bound Isaac his son, and laid him on the altar upon the wood.*
>
> *Genesis 22:9*

Isaac had age and strength on his side and could have easily resisted his elderly father. Yet not once do we see Isaac try to out run or overpower his father, something I believe he could have done with relative ease. Neither does Isaac try to resist his own imminent death.

This situation is often referred to as *a test of Abraham's faith*, but I also believe it was a test of Isaac's faith. From Isaac's reaction, *or maybe I should say his non-reaction*, to being bound and laid on the altar on wood it is obvious that he knew something. Isaac believed what his father had said; Isaac knew that *God would provide Himself a lamb for a burnt offering:*

> *⁸And Abraham said, My son, GOD WILL PROVIDE HIMSELF A LAMB for a burnt offering: so they went both of them together.*
>
> Genesis 22:8

Not being funny but has it ever dawned on you that, even though Isaac was almost *slaughtered* by his father, the scriptures do not record that when he was unbound and taken off the altar, Isaac ran for his life down the mount, jumped on the donkey, and tried to escape from his father? ABRAHAM AND ISAAC RETURNED TOGETHER!

Isaac did not moan and groan about the experience, he did not inform *the local police* about what his father had tried to do, and he sure did not dash off to *the local newspaper* to sell his story. The truth is, Isaac willingly submitted because he had grown to know God. Isaac had a personal faith in God; the same faith Abraham had in God's power to resurrect his son was also inculcated in Isaac.

Somehow this comes as no surprise because over the years Isaac had seen God in action, albeit through his father, Abraham. Isaac's trust in God was growing daily. Among other things Isaac's parents, Abraham and Sarah, would most likely have told him of how The Almighty God had promised him to them, even though they were old and well stricken in age; even though Sarah had passed the age of child birth. Sarah may have even told Isaac how she had laughed at the thought of her bearing a child at such an old age, but as usual God had the last laugh. *"I guess that is why He called you laughter"*.

---

## Isaac was involved in a near death experience

---

So, when Abraham said *God will provide himself a lamb* ISAAC KNEW GOD WOULD, and had faith in The Almighty God even in the face of death. Here, Isaac's faith, his willingness and obedience were tested by God and I believe this was where the foundation of his personal relationship with The Almighty God was laid.

So, even though it is often said that Isaac did not experience anything his father Abraham had not already experienced, he actually did. Isaac was involved in a *"NEAR DEATH EXPERIENCE"*; an experience that opened his eyes to the provision of The Most High God. It was a personal experience in which Isaac came to know God as *Jehovah Jireh {another face of God}*

## A personal relationship
Proof of Isaac's relationship with God is seen when The Almighty God turns around Rebekah's barren situation. Isaac *knew* that there was nothing his God could not do so when he asked believing he received what he had asked for:

> [21] *And Isaac intreated the LORD for his wife, because she was barren: and the LORD was intreated of him, and Rebekah his wife conceived.*
>
> *Genesis 25:21*

Also, evidence of what Isaac shared with God is seen in

Genesis chapter 26. Here God cuts a covenant with Isaac. As Isaac stepped out in faith by *NOT* going to Egypt, God promised to be with him. God also reaffirmed the promises he made to his father, Abraham:

> *2And the LORD appeared unto him, and said, Go not down into Egypt; dwell in the land which I shall tell thee of:*
> *3Sojourn in this land, and I will be with thee, and will bless thee; for unto thee, and unto thy seed, I will give all these countries, and I will perform the oath which I sware unto Abraham thy father;*
> *4And I will make thy seed to multiply as the stars of heaven, and will give unto thy seed all these countries; and in thy seed shall all the nations of the earth be blessed;*
>
> *Genesis 26:2-4*

Isaac's hearing and obeying God's voice is witnessed again and again. Isaac stayed out of Egypt in a land called Gerar, sowed in the midst of famine and reaped a hundredfold in the same year simply because, by faith, he obeyed a divine instruction. It did not matter which well he dug in the land of Gerar; whenever Isaac dug a well he hit water simply because he was walking in obedience to the word he had received from the Lord.

God blessed Isaac so much that Abimelech, king of the Philistines, could not help but notice. In fact, Abimelech was so fear stricken that he cut a covenant with Isaac to ensure the safety of his people:

> *26Then Abimelech went to him from Gerar, and Ahuzzath one of his friends, and Phichol the chief captain of his army.*
> *27And Isaac said unto them, Wherefore come ye to me, seeing ye hate me, and have sent me away from you?*
> *28And they said, We saw certainly that the LORD was with thee: and we said, Let there be now an oath betwixt us, even betwixt us and thee, and let us make a covenant with thee;*
> *29That thou wilt do us no hurt, as we have not touched thee, and as we have done unto thee nothing but good, and have*

*sent thee away in peace: thou art now the blessed of the LORD.*

---

### *...though Isaac's relationship with God had its roots in Abraham, Isaac still had to know God for himself*

---

Isaac was born in the Promised Land, lived in the Promised Land and died in the Promised Land; Isaac was a child of promise. The scriptures show that Isaac's characteristic was to inherit; *...Abraham gave all that he had unto Isaac {Genesis 25:5}.* However, one thing that we cannot take away from Isaac is that he knew The Almighty God.

So agreed, though Isaac's relationship with God had its roots in Abraham, Isaac still had to know God for himself. That was the only way he could step out in faith. Isaac had an intimate relationship with God. He knew God's voice and because of his willingness and obedience he ate the good of the land.

# FATHER
## OF
# THE TWELVE TRIBES

We all remember Jacob; the man who wrestled with God, had his name changed to Israel by God, and whose twelve sons were the twelve patriarchs of the twelve tribes of God's chosen people. Not bad, but let us briefly take a closer look at the pages of Jacob's life.

Jacob was the younger of the *miracle* twins born to Isaac and Rebekah {*remember, Rebekah was actually barren – Genesis 25:21*}. At birth he came out grasping his older brother's heel, which explains the reason behind his name. Jacob means *"one who grasps by the heel"*, *"heel-grabber"* or *"supplanter"*. How interesting it is that, as Jacob grew older, these meanings were actually characteristics of his life.

About a fourth of the book of Genesis has something to say about the life of Jacob, and in these chapters we notice that his life was characterized by scheming, manipulation and getting what he wanted through the *necessary* means. Jacob was a deceitful, untrustworthy and devious man.

In the sight of his brother Esau, Jacob was a crook. But then God says that, apart from being the God of Abraham and Isaac, HE IS ALSO THE GOD OF JACOB. Does this mean that God actually had a part to play in the life of *crafty old Jacob?*

## God's inversion plan

By tradition the firstborn, the eldest, had the right of inheritance, and would, by default, rule over the younger members of the family. But with Esau and Jacob there was a bit of a twist. God had an *inversion* plan which He revealed to Rebekah in Genesis chapter 25;

> [22] *And the children struggled together within her; and she said, If it be so, why am I thus? And she went to enquire of the LORD.*
> [23] *And the LORD said unto her, Two nations are in thy womb, and two manner of people shall be separated from thy bowels; and the one people shall be stronger than the other people; and THE ELDER SHALL SERVE THE YOUNGER.*
>
> *Genesis 25:22-23*

God spoke to Rebekah concerning the twins in her womb and He made her realise that the younger twin would inherit *the blessing of the firstborn.* With this insight it makes perfect sense why Rebekah loved Jacob *{Genesis 25:28}* and, within her own understanding, was willing to lay down her life to ensure that what God had told her concerning Jacob came to pass *{Genesis 27:13}.*

Two significant events seem to set the ball rolling when it comes to Jacob's life. These have to do with *"the birthright"* and *"the blessing"*.

## The birthright

Jacob was busy cooking up some lentil stew when Esau, his elder brother, walks in after a day of hunting game in the fields. Esau was hungry, so hungry that he seems to think that he is about to die. I get the feeling that this was a bit of an exaggeration on Esau's part. What would he have done if Jacob was not cooking and there was nothing to eat; *would he have died?* Somehow I believe Esau could have waited but it seemed like Jacob's lentil stew was irresistible. Jacob realising that he had Esau where he wanted him seizes the opportunity and offers Esau some lentil stew in exchange for his birthright:

> *[31] And Jacob said, Sell me this day thy birthright.*
> *[32] And Esau said, Behold, I am at the point to die: and what profit shall this birthright do to me?*
> *[33] And Jacob said, Swear to me this day; and he sware unto him: and he sold his birthright unto Jacob.*
> *[34] Then Jacob gave Esau bread and pottage of lentiles; and he did eat and drink, and rose up, and went his way: thus Esau despised his birthright.*
>
> *Genesis 25:31-34*

---

*For a moment of pleasure Esau gave up the material and spiritual blessings that were rightly his*

---

The birthright meant a double portion of the paternal inheritance *{Deuteronomy 21:17}*, as well as the headship of the family. Since, by default, it belonged to the firstborn it implied that the younger members of the family would serve the firstborn. However, as Isaac's firstborn, Esau's birthright included a lot more than material blessings. It was loaded with spiritual realities; *the blessings of Abraham*. Being the one that Isaac loved so dearly *{Genesis 25:28}* Esau most likely knew the importance of his birthright; Isaac would have shared this with him.

Esau's birthright was linked to the promises that God had given his grandfather, Abraham. *One of these promises was*

*the promise of the promised seed; the promise of the Messiah.*
Abraham's promises had been passed down to Isaac and
they were now about to rest on Esau. However, in Esau's
words, *"Behold, I am at the point to die: and what profit shall
this birthright do to me?"* we see that Esau disdains his
birthright. Once Jacob handed over the bread and lentil
stew Esau did not look back; he simply ate, drank, rose up
and went his way. *Esau lost everything that day and simply
could not be bothered. So sad!*

For a moment of pleasure Esau gave up the material and
spiritual blessings that were rightly his. Even though Esau
knew how precious his birthright was, his actions show
that he placed little or no value on it. This was a sign of
the value Esau actually placed on God, and explains why
Esau is described as a *godless* man in Hebrews chapter 12;

> [16] *That no one may become guilty of sexual vice, or become A
> PROFANE (GODLESS AND SACRILEGIOUS) PERSON AS ESAU
> DID, who sold his own birthright for a single meal.*
>
> Hebrews 12:16 {AMP}

Jacob on the other hand did not have to think twice about
what he wanted in return for his lentil stew. He valued
the birthright greatly. Maybe Jacob was not exactly the
*straightest of men* but in his heart he valued the things of
God. He understood the importance of the birthright and
did not take it lightly. *He wanted it!*

## The blessing
The story of the much talked about *blessing* is found in
Genesis chapter 27. Isaac was close to giving up the ghost
and asks Esau, his firstborn, to cook him his favourite
meal so that *he may eat* after which *his soul would bless
Esau before he died.* But Rebekah, the mother of Esau and
Jacob, had a plan up her sleeve. Hearing her husband's

request, and maybe remembering what God had told her in Genesis chapter 25:23, she decided the time had come to *lend God a helping hand {not exactly the right move but...}.* Jacob, with the help of his mother, proceeded to deceive Isaac into believing that he was Esau so that he would receive Esau's blessing, *the blessing of the firstborn.*

---

### *...the blessing of the firstborn was always meant to rest on the bearer of the birthright*

---

From the dialogue in Genesis chapter 27:18-27, we see that Isaac was obviously very suspicious. Firstly, the food was cooked in record time. Then when Isaac asks, "*How is it that thou hast found it so quickly, my son?*" Jacob's response, "*Because the LORD thy God brought it to me*", must have sounded a bit too spiritual for his godless firstborn. Isaac, still uncertain, then touches and smells his son. This seemed to confirm that the son that stood before him was Esau, his firstborn. Finally, Isaac asks, "*Art thou my very son Esau?*" and without a tinge of hesitation deceitful Jacob responded, "*I am*". The voice Isaac heard seemed to belong to Jacob but after a touch, a smell and a lie detection test he fell for Jacob's deceit.

Something that must not be overlooked in all this is that the blessing of the firstborn was always meant to rest on the bearer of the birthright. Isaac most likely did not know that Esau had sold out to Jacob until Esau revealed it:

> <sup>36</sup>*And he said, Is not he rightly named Jacob? for he hath supplanted me these two times: he took away my birthright; and, behold, now he hath taken away my blessing. And he said, Hast thou not reserved a blessing for me?*
>
> *Genesis 27:36*

So, even though Jacob and his mother had deceived Isaac,

God in His sovereignty still ensured that Isaac did the right thing; *he gave the blessing of the firstborn to the bearer of the birthright.*

> [26] *And his father Isaac said unto him, Come near now, and kiss me, my son.*
> [27] *And he came near, and kissed him: and he smelled the smell of his raiment, and blessed him, and said, See, the smell of my son is as the smell of a field which the LORD hath blessed:*
> [28] *Therefore God give thee of the dew of heaven, and the fatness of the earth, and plenty of corn and wine:*
> [29] *Let people serve thee, and nations bow down to thee: be lord over thy brethren, and let thy mother's sons bow down to thee: cursed be every one that curseth thee, and blessed be he that blesseth thee.*
>
> *Genesis 27:26-29*

It is interesting to see that the blessing that Isaac had intended for Esau, *but which he ended up proclaiming over Jacob,* was mainly a *material* blessing; *the dew of heaven, the fatness of the earth, corn and wine, the respect of nations, lord over his brethren and so on.* Suddenly it all makes sense; even though from scripture we see that Isaac loved Esau, he also knew that the son he loved was not a God fearing man. Isaac was a Godly man who had a personal relationship with Jehovah so he knew he could not proclaim *the blessing of Abraham* over Esau. The blessing of Abraham was always reserved for Jacob as we see in Genesis chapter 28:

> [1] *And Isaac called Jacob, and blessed him, and charged him, and said unto him, Thou shalt not take a wife of the daughters of Canaan.*
> [2] *Arise, go to Padanaram, to the house of Bethuel thy mother's father; and take thee a wife from thence of the daughers of Laban thy mother's brother.*
> [3] *AND GOD ALMIGHTY BLESS THEE, AND MAKE THEE FRUITFUL, AND MULTIPLY THEE, THAT THOU MAYEST BE*

*A MULTITUDE OF PEOPLE;*
*⁴AND GIVE THEE THE BLESSING OF ABRAHAM, TO THEE,*
*AND TO THY SEED WITH THEE; THAT THOU MAYEST*
*INHERIT THE LAND WHEREIN THOU ART A STRANGER,*
*WHICH GOD GAVE UNTO ABRAHAM.*

*Genesis 28:1-4*

---

## ...God saw that Jacob had a heart that sought after Him

---

I wonder how Esau felt knowing that his father had blessed Jacob with Abraham's blessing. *"Hmm, so the old man still had that blessing up his sleeve and he could only bless me with remnants"*. He must have been fuming, but deep down inside he would have known that Isaac could never have proclaimed Abraham's blessing over him. I believe Isaac always had a plan; to give the *material* blessing to Esau and the spiritual blessing solely to Jacob. If this was not the case Isaac would have proclaimed the spiritual blessing over Esau after he had been deceived. Instead Isaac *trembled* and declared that he had *blessed Jacob and Jacob SHALL be blessed*, almost implying that *what was yours I have given to your younger brother and there is nothing I can do about it.*

Despite all his deceitfulness and scheming, God seemed to love Jacob deeply. Not as if Jacob's ways were pleasing to God but I believe God saw that Jacob had a heart that sought after Him. *He wanted the birthright which implied that his heart was hungry for spiritual things.* So, when God says, *"Jacob I loved, but Esau I hated"*, He was simply placing a stamp on the fact that HE, *and not a man or woman, CHOSE JACOB.*

So, Jacob runs out with the birthright and a two-fold

blessing. But, in all this a question that one cannot help but ask is *"did Jacob even have a relationship of any sort with God?"*

## The dream

After blessing Jacob with *the blessing*, Isaac commands Jacob to leave Canaan so as to find a wife in Padanaram in the land of Haran. This, once again, was orchestrated by Rebekah so as to shield Jacob from Esau's anger *{Genesis 27:42-46}*. This marked the beginning of a twenty year journey in which the seeds of deceitfulness that Jacob had sown seemed to catch up with him *{the Laban experience!}*. It also marked the beginning of a personal relationship with *Jehovah Rohi {Genesis 48:15}*.

Jacob's first personal experience with God is recorded in Genesis chapter 28 when Jacob was on his way to Laban's place. The sun had set so Jacob decided to spend the night in a place where he could only use stones for a pillow. While Jacob was sleeping God appeared to him in a dream:

> *[12]And he dreamed, and behold a ladder set up on the earth, and the top of it reached to heaven: and behold the angels of God ascending and descending on it.*
> *[13]And, behold, the LORD stood above it, and said, I am the LORD God of Abraham thy father, and the God of Isaac: the land whereon thou liest, to thee will I give it, and to thy seed;*
> *[14]And thy seed shall be as the dust of the earth, and thou shalt spread abroad to the west, and to the east, and to the north, and to the south: and in thee and in thy seed shall all the families of the earth be blessed.*
>
> *Genesis 28:12-14*

From scripture, this was also the first time that God had personally spoken to Jacob and, in case Jacob had any doubts, God confirmed the blessings that his father had proclaimed over his life in verses 3 & 4. But then, God also adds a little extra:

> <sup>15</sup>*And, behold, I am with thee, and will keep thee in all places whither thou goest, and will bring thee again into this land; for I will not leave thee, until I have done that which I have spoken to thee of.*

*Genesis 28:15*

These were not words that God had spoken to either his grandfather Abraham or his father Isaac. These words were specifically for Jacob and they formed the foundation of this divine relationship. At a crucial time, when most likely Jacob was feeling a little lonely and isolated, God brought comfort and hope by telling Jacob that He would take care of him, protect him, lead him and that He would never leave him. God was telling Jacob that He would be his sole provider; *in other words, God was telling Jacob that He would be his Shepherd.*

---

### *God's promise to Jacob was totally God-centered; an unconditional promise of blessing*

---

When Jacob finally woke up he was afraid. He had just experienced something he had never experienced before; *the very presence of the Most High God!* After a time of worship he called the place Bethel, *the house of God.* However, even after such an experience we again see a manifestation of Jacob's carnal nature when he makes his vow to God:

> <sup>20</sup>*And Jacob vowed a vow, saying, If God will be with me, and will keep me in this way that I go, and will give me bread to eat, and raiment to put on,*
> <sup>21</sup>*So that I come again to my father's house in peace; then shall the LORD be my God:*
> <sup>22</sup>*And this stone, which I have set for a pillar, shall be God's house: and of all that thou shalt give me I will surely give*

*the tenth unto thee.*

This was almost like Jacob cutting a deal with God; he even promised God a tenth of what God gave him in the first place if God made good on His promise. God's promise to Jacob was totally God-centered; an unconditional promise of blessing. In return Jacob's vow to God was very conditional and purely *Jacob-centered; "… If God will be with ME, and will keep ME in this way that I go, and will give ME…"* One could say that Jacob still had an issue with submission, but all that soon changed when God brought Uncle Laban into his life.

## The Laban experience

Laban was Rebekah's brother, Jacob's uncle, so one could say it would have been safe for Jacob to assume that he was in safe hands. However, Jacob would soon realise that Laban was a swindler in his own right. **When he fell in love with Laban's daughter Rachel**, Jacob struck a seven year *labour deal* with Laban in return for her hand in marriage *{Genesis 29:18}*. After Jacob had fulfilled the seven years Laban threw a wedding party; Jacob most likely took a little excess and did not realise that his father-in-law had done a wedding night switch:

> <sup>22</sup>*And Laban gathered together all the men of the place, and made a feast.*
> <sup>23</sup>*And it came to pass in the evening, that he took Leah his daughter, and brought her to him; and he went in unto her.*
> <sup>24</sup>*And Laban gave unto his daughter Leah Zilpah his maid for an handmaid.*
> <sup>25</sup>*And it came to pass, that in the morning, behold, it was Leah: and he said to Laban, What is this thou hast done unto me? did not I serve with thee for Rachel? wherefore then hast thou beguiled me?*
> <sup>26</sup>*And Laban said, It must not be so done in our country, to give the younger before the firstborn.*

> <sup>27</sup>*Fulfil her week, and we will give thee this also for the service which thou shalt serve with me yet seven other years.*
> <sup>28</sup>*And Jacob did so, and fulfilled her week: and he gave him Rachel his daughter to wife also.*
> <sup>29</sup>*And Laban gave to Rachel his daughter Bilhah his handmaid to be her maid.*
>
> 

*Genesis 29:22-29*

Of course Laban knew what he was up to from the very first day of the deal but Jacob fell for his deceit. *Jacob must have thought he was suffering from a bout of déjà vu, the only difference being that this time around he was on the receiving end!*

Well, another seven years of hard labour went by and Rachel's dowry was finally paid. But it did not end there. After fourteen long years and finally getting his hands on the lady of his dreams it turned out that Rachel was actually barren:

> <sup>31</sup>*And when the LORD saw that Leah was hated, he opened her womb: BUT RACHEL WAS BARREN.*
>
> 

*Genesis 29:31*

*{So first of all Abraham's wife, Sarah had a dead womb, then Isaac's wife, Rebekah was barren and now Jacob's beloved finds herself in the same situation. But, when God opened up their wombs they brought forth Isaac, Jacob and Joseph respectively; men that God used to manifest His plan for His chosen people: the Israelites!}*

---

### *Laban knew that the reason why the LORD had blessed him was because of Jacob's presence*

---

God finally gave Rachel the fruit of the womb and it was after this that Jacob decided that it was time to return home *{Genesis 30:22-25}*. However, with a father-in-law like Laban that was never going to be straightforward. Laban knew that the reason why the LORD had blessed him was *because of Jacob's presence {Genesis 30:27}*. Laban did not intend to let Jacob go without a *"fight"*. Laban begged Jacob to stay, with the added incentive of a pay rise to be set by Jacob himself, but Jacob was not keen on this. Instead he chose to put his trust in the Lord.

> *31And he said, What shall I give thee? And Jacob said, Thou shalt not give me any thing: if thou wilt do this thing for me, I will again feed and keep thy flock.*
> *32I will pass through all thy flock to day, removing from thence all the speckled and spotted cattle, and all the brown cattle among the sheep, and the spotted and speckled among the goats: and of such shall be my hire.*
> *33SO SHALL MY RIGHTEOUSNESS ANSWER FOR ME IN TIME TO COME, when it shall come for my hire before thy face: every one that is not speckled and spotted among the goats, and brown among the sheep, that shall be counted stolen with me.*
>
> Genesis 30:31-33

Jacob decided to enter into a flock agreement with Laban. It was an agreement that seemed to favour Laban immensely because removing the spotted and striped which were in the flock would lessen the chances of other spotted or striped animals being conceived, as they would not mate with the rest of the flock. So, it came as no surprise when Laban embraced the agreement with open arms. *After all, with Jacob tending the unspotted, unstriped and unspeckled flock what could go wrong?*

> *34And Laban said, Behold, I would it might be according to thy word.*
>
> Genesis 30:34

It has been said that Jacob placing himself in an almost impossible situation to prosper and then using a *"rod concept"* on the unspotted, unstriped and unspeckled flock was another one of his schemes, but I tend to disagree. There is something about all this that is simply divine. Why would Jacob come up with an agreement that did not favour him? What gave him the boldness to utter words such as, *"So shall my righteousness answer for me in time to come, when it shall come for my hire before thy face"*? Where did the inspiration for the rod concept come from, because before now no such concept is mentioned in the scriptures? Why was Jacob so sure that the concept would work? Who else could turn this almost impossible situation into a total success?

> [43] *And the man increased exceedingly, and had much cattle, and maidservants, and menservants, and camels, and asses.*
>
> *Genesis 30:43*

Remember God's promise to Jacob? *God promised that He would be with Jacob; God promised He would look after Jacob wherever he went; God promised never to leave Jacob until He had brought him back into the Promised Land. God had promised to be Jacob's shepherd.* Jacob had witnessed the constant manifestation of God's promise in his life. So, it does not take a genius to see that Jacob's trust in God had grown over the years. The truth is Laban knew that the hand of God was upon Jacob's life, and Jacob definitely was not confused about this truth:

> [1] *And he heard THE WORDS OF LABAN'S SONS, saying, Jacob hath taken away all that was our father's; and of that which was our father's hath he gotten all this glory.*
> [5] *And said unto them, I see your father's countenance, that it is not toward me as before; BUT THE GOD OF MY FATHER HATH BEEN WITH ME.*
> [7] *And your father hath deceived me, and changed my wages*

*ten times; BUT GOD SUFFERED HIM NOT TO HURT ME.*
*⁹Thus GOD HATH TAKEN AWAY THE CATTLE OF YOUR*
*FATHER, AND GIVEN THEM TO ME.*

*Genesis 31:1,5,7,9*

It is interesting that there had been no mention of Laban having a son, not to talk of sons. Actually, it is almost assumed that Laban did not have any sons in the first place. So, how come this is the first time the scriptures mention Laban's sons? Taking a closer look at verses 27 & 30 of Genesis chapter 30 seems to shed some light:

> *²⁷And Laban said unto him, I pray thee, if I have found favour in thine eyes, tarry: for I have learned by experience that the LORD hath blessed me for thy sake.*
> *³⁰For it was little which thou hadst before I came, and it is now increased unto a multitude; AND THE LORD HATH BLESSED THEE SINCE MY COMING: and now when shall I provide for mine own house also?*

*Genesis 30:27,30*

---

### *...Jacob's experience with Laban helped build his trust in The Most High God*

---

We see that before the arrival of Jacob Laban did not have much of an inheritance, and like Jacob rightly told his uncle, *"...you had little before I came...,"* However, as Laban's *"little"* became *"a multitude"*, **due to his association with Jacob**, he found himself having an inheritance that he could pass on. Back in the day a man's inheritance could only be passed on to his sons *{even though that changed when the daughters of Zelophehad presented their situation to Moses in Numbers 27:1-11}*. So, now it begins to make sense why Laban's son's had suddenly come into the picture.

Till now there was probably no need to mention Laban's boys anyway. I imagine them being a bunch of lazy lads who had their eyes on their father's wealth. This could explain their agitation when they realised that their father's wealth, *their inheritance*, was dwindling. When what was *rightfully* theirs seemed to be disappearing because of Jacob's presence, it was time for them to speak up. *{If only they understood that Jacob's presence was the reason why they had an inheritance in the first place!}*.

When Jacob overheard Laban's sons imply that he had stolen their inheritance, and also noticed that his favour level with his father-in-law had dropped considerably, Jacob needed direction and once again The Lord, as promised, stepped in:

> *³And the LORD said unto Jacob, Return unto the land of thy fathers, and to thy kindred; AND I WILL BE WITH THEE.*
>
> *Genesis 31:3*

After twenty long years it was finally time for Jacob to leave. To Rachel and Leah this was not an issue but Jacob knew that getting past their father would once again pose a problem. However, Jacob trusted God and was willing to obey His word; compared to obeying God, the fear of Laban meant nothing. So, Jacob, *with all he had*, decided to do a *runner*. When Laban heard about what Jacob had done he gathered the *troops* and pursued Jacob. Laban planned to kill Jacob but yet again we see the hand of God move on Jacob's behalf:

> *²⁴And God came to Laban the Syrian in a dream by night, and said unto him, TAKE HEED THAT THOU SPEAK NOT TO JACOB EITHER GOOD OR BAD.*
> *²⁹It is in the power of my hand to do you hurt: but THE GOD OF YOUR FATHER SPAKE UNTO ME YESTERNIGHT, saying, Take thou heed that thou speak not to Jacob either good or bad.*
>
> *Genesis 31:24,29*

Jacob's experience with Laban was no coincidence. It was planned by God. Jacob the schemer, the deceitful one met his match in his uncle Laban; Jacob was unable to beat Laban at his own game. Laban deceived, cheated and almost killed Jacob, and Jacob seemed to take it all on the chin.

> <sup>38</sup>*This twenty years have I been with thee; thy ewes and thy she goats have not cast their young, and the rams of thy flock have I not eaten.*
>
> <sup>39</sup>*That which was torn of beasts I brought not unto thee; I bare the loss of it; of my hand didst thou require it, whether stolen by day, or stolen by night.*
>
> <sup>40</sup>*Thus I was; in the day the drought consumed me, and the frost by night; and my sleep departed from mine eyes.*
>
> <sup>41</sup>*Thus have I been twenty years in thy house; I served thee fourteen years for thy two daughters, and six years for thy cattle: and thou hast changed my wages ten times.*
>
> <sup>42</sup>*EXCEPT THE GOD OF MY FATHER, THE GOD OF ABRAHAM, AND THE FEAR OF ISAAC, HAD BEEN WITH ME, SURELY THOU HADST SENT ME AWAY NOW EMPTY. God hath seen mine affliction and the labour of my hands, and rebuked thee yesternight.*
>
> *Genesis 31:38-42*

Laban gave Jacob a lesson in submission that he would not forget in a hurry. More importantly, Jacob's experience with Laban helped build his trust in The Most High God; *it made Jacob realise that God, and God alone, was his shepherd.*

## Face to face

As Jacob started the journey home it dawned on him that he would have to travel through Esau's land. Despite coming across the angels of God, *a guarantee that God's presence was with him,* Jacob once again exercised human wisdom by offering his brother a bribe, but unsurprisingly this failed. Esau wasn't even tempted! Seeing Esau's response Jacob was gripped with fear and it was in fear that he called on God *{Genesis 32:9-12}.* From scripture this was the first time Jacob prayed to God, his bargaining nature seemed to have been replaced with humility. But somehow he just could not resist his scheming ways.

---

*For Jacob to obtain the blessing he had to drop all pride, manipulation and self-reliance*

---

Jacob decides to send multiple bribes to his approaching brother hoping that he would ultimately touch his heart but somehow he must have known that it was all in vain. Preparing for the worst Jacob sends his family and all his belongings to the other side of the brook while he stayed to face his fate. It was time for the *encounter*. However, it turned out not to be with Esau but with Someone else; *God in human form.*

> <sup>24</sup>*And Jacob was left alone; and there wrestled a man with him until the breaking of the day.*
> <sup>25</sup>*And when he saw that he prevailed not against him, he touched the hollow of his thigh; and the hollow of Jacob's thigh was out of joint, as he wrestled with him.*
> <sup>26</sup>*And he said, Let me go, for the day breaketh. And he said, I will not let thee go, except thou bless me.*
> <sup>27</sup>*And he said unto him, What is thy name? And he said, Jacob.*
> <sup>28</sup>*And he said, Thy name shall be called no more Jacob, but Israel: for as a prince hast thou power with God and with men, and hast prevailed.*
> <sup>29</sup>*And Jacob asked him, and said, Tell me, I pray thee, thy name. And he said, Wherefore is it that thou dost ask after my name? And he blessed him there.*
> <sup>30</sup>*And Jacob called the name of the place Peniel: for I have seen God face to face, and my life is preserved.*
> <sup>31</sup>*And as he passed over Penuel the sun rose upon him, and he halted upon his thigh.*
>
> *Genesis 32:24-31*

This wrestling bout, initiated by God Himself, marked the turning point in Jacob's spiritual life. Until now Jacob lived up to his name; he had schemed, deceived, cheated and bargained, even with God {Genesis 28:20-22}. Jacob still thought he could use his carnal methods to get spiritual blessings as it seemed to work in times past, but his thinking was about to change.

All the while Jacob must have felt that Esau was the obstacle preventing him from entering Canaan, and into the blessings of God. The truth is that Esau did not have the *power* to prevent Jacob from obtaining the blessing of God. The only person that stood in the way of Jacob's blessing in the land of Canaan was *The Giver* of the blessing; God Himself! The blessing of God could only be obtained from God and not by the arm of flesh. For Jacob to obtain the blessing he had to drop all pride, manipulation and self-reliance.

One gets the impression that Jacob must have been doing most of the holding on in this wrestling bout, while God was more or less *trying to cut him loose*. However, when God realised that Jacob was rather persistent He touched him. This touch turned Jacob into a cripple but though he could no longer fight, Jacob still hung on to God with all his might. In Hosea chapter 12:3-5 we see that Jacob *sought the blessing with weeping*. In the past, Jacob never really felt the need to trust solely in God because in his eyes he thought he was clever. However, Jacob was now experiencing a change; from being *self-sufficient* to being *totally dependent. Jacob had to cling in helpless dependence to The Giver of the blessing to receive the blessing.*

---

*At Peniel, the place where Jacob saw God face to face, he realized that God alone, not his power or might, held the key to spiritual blessings*

---

In the midst of this encounter God changes Jacob's name to Israel. From the scriptures we see that ISRAEL means *"contender with God"*. However, the name ISRAEL is also said to be a compound of two words: **SARAR**, which means to *"rule"*, *"reign"* or *"act"*, and **EL**, which means *"God"*. Considering that when it comes to Hebrew names I am told that God sometimes is not the object of the verb but the subject, ISRAEL could actually mean, *"God rules"*. At Peniel, *the place where Jacob saw God face to face*, he realized that God alone, not his power or might, held the key to spiritual blessings. At Peniel, Jacob came to understand that the sovereign God truly rules and He needs no human assistance. Jacob's new name would forever remind him of this.

## The Lord my shepherd
In Jacob's old age he speaks of the relationship that he shared with God:

> <sup>15</sup>*And he blessed Joseph, and said, God, before whom my fathers Abraham and Isaac did walk, THE GOD WHICH FED ME ALL MY LIFE LONG UNTO THIS DAY,*

> *Genesis 48:15*

In the Amplified Bible the later part of this verse reads, *"... Who has [been my Shepherd and has led and] fed me from the time I came into being until this day"*. Here Israel, formerly known as Jacob, acknowledges God as *Jehovah Rohi*, the Lord his Shepherd. A look at the Sheep-Shepherd relationship sheds more light on what Israel had come to understand.

Sheep do not exactly fall into the category of smart animals. They happen to be one of the few animals who, if left alone, will totally destroy their pasture. They are easily terrified and are prone to wandering off. Sheep require constant attention and they depend on the shepherd for all their needs.

The shepherd has the responsibility of caring for the sheep. He feeds them, tends to their wounds, calms them if they get agitated and rescues them whenever the need arises. The shepherd keeps the flock together and when necessary he uses his rod and staff to keep them in check. In the eye of the shepherd each sheep is of equal importance. *If one of the sheep left the flock and got lost the shepherd would not rest until it was found. The shepherd is the SOLE PROVIDER for his flock; he provides their every need.* This explains why Israel refers to God as his shepherd.

In many ways Israel {Jacob} could relate to the sheep; *prone to wandering off and constantly requiring attention.* However, because of the presence of The Shepherd in his life he had survived the *"dark valleys"* and his soul had constantly been restored. Israel {Jacob} had tasted the green pastures and drank from the still waters; he had also experienced The Shepherd's rod and staff. Even when he seemed to be running the show in his own might, The Shepherd in His sovereignty ensured that His goodness and mercy followed him. Israel {Jacob} had come to realise that *The Shepherd had led him and fed him from the time he came into being until this day.* Jacob had come to acknowledge *Jehovah Rohi* as his sole provider.

---

*Jacob had come to acknowledge Jehovah Rohi as his sole provider*

---

## The prophecy
When Isaac was about to die he spoke a blessing into the lives of his sons, Esau and Jacob. In other words, Isaac

invoked God's favour upon Esau and Jacob. However, the situation was a little different when it came to Jacob and his sons.

> ¹*And Jacob called unto his sons, and said, Gather yourselves together, that I may tell you THAT WHICH SHALL BEFALL YOU IN THE LAST DAYS.*

*Genesis 49:1*

In Genesis chapter 49:1, just before he gave up the ghost, we see that Jacob did not bless his sons, he prophesied into their lives. Jacob foretold the future of his sons by divine inspiration. This, once again, was a manifestation of the relationship Jacob shared with God. Taking a closer look at Genesis chapter 49 something interesting comes to light.

After gathering his sons around his death bed, Jacob began to prophesy into their lives. He started off with Reuben, his firstborn, and then moved on to Simeon and Levi. Thus far the words that had proceeded from Jacob's lips were not exactly pleasing to the ear so you can just imagine Judah *trembling* a little when his father called out his name:

> ⁸*Judah, thou art he whom thy brethren shall praise: thy hand shall be in the neck of thine enemies; thy father's children shall bow down before thee.*
> ⁹*Judah is a lion's whelp: from the prey, my son, thou art gone up: he stooped down, he couched as a lion, and as an old lion; who shall rouse him up?*
> ¹⁰*THE SCEPTRE SHALL NOT DEPART FROM JUDAH, NOR A LAWGIVER FROM BETWEEN HIS FEET, UNTIL SHILOH COME; AND UNTO HIM SHALL THE GATHERING OF THE PEOPLE BE.*
> ¹¹*Binding his foal unto the vine, and his ass's colt unto the choice vine; he washed his garments in wine, and his clothes in the blood of grapes:*

<sup></sup>*¹²His eyes shall be red with wine, and his teeth white with milk.*

*Genesis 49:8-12*

Judah would be praised by his brothers *{after all, his name does signify praise!}*. Judah would be honoured by his father's children. In a sense, *the birthright, which Reuben had forfeited, was now being handed to Judah.* Judah would be victorious and have dominion. Judah would be like a couching lion; one that would enjoy the satisfaction of his power and success. However, the icing on the cake comes in verse 10. **JUDAH WOULD BE THE ROYAL TRIBE; THE TRIBE FROM WHICH THE MESSIAH, THE PRINCE OF PEACE, WOULD COME.**

So, as Jacob, now known as Israel, lay on his death bed God revealed to him specifics about the coming of the Messiah, Jesus Christ. **SIMPLY AMAZING!**

# ISRAEL'S MEDIATOR

The Israelites had dwelt in Egypt for a number of years; they were fruitful and had multiplied greatly. In fact, Egypt was filled with Israelites:

> *⁷And the children of Israel were fruitful, and increased abundantly, and multiplied, and waxed exceeding mighty; and the land was filled with them.*
>
> *Exodus 1:7*

Thanks to Joseph, the son of Israel, the Israelites were having a lovely time in Egypt; you could almost say that it had become their *home*. But this changed when an Egyptian king who did not know Joseph came to power. Realising that the children of Israel by far outnumbered the *actual owners* of the land he decided it was time to do something about it. His reign marked the beginning of slavery for the children of Israel:

> *⁸Now there arose up a new king over Egypt, which knew not Joseph.*
> *⁹And he said unto his people, Behold, the people of the children of Israel are more and mightier than we:*
> *¹⁰Come on, let us deal wisely with them; lest they multiply,*

*and it come to pass, that, when there falleth out any war, they join also unto our enemies, and fight against us, and so get them up out of the land.*

*¹¹ Therefore they did set over them taskmasters to afflict them with their burdens. And they built for Pharaoh treasure cities, Pithom and Raamses.*

*Exodus 1:8-11*

Pharaoh soon realised that the more he made the lives of the Israelites *bitter with hard bondage* the more they grew and multiplied. So, to slow down the rate at which the children of Israel grew in the land Pharaoh decreed that all Hebrew male children should be killed. It was during this time that Moses was born.

## From basket to palace

Moses' mother *Jochebed* raised him for the first three months against the *law of the land* but then she could no longer hide him. So as to give Moses a chance of survival *Jochebed* placed her son in a basket and put him in the Nile. Moses' sister Miriam watched as the basket floated down the river and witnessed Pharaoh's daughter pick Moses out from among the reeds of the Nile. What happened next is simply the hand of God in motion:

*⁵ And the daughter of Pharaoh came down to wash herself at the river; and her maidens walked along by the river's side; and when she saw the ark among the flags, she sent her maid to fetch it.*

*⁶ And when she had opened it, she saw the child: and, behold, the babe wept. And she had compassion on him, and said, This is one of the Hebrews' children.*

*⁷ Then said his sister to Pharaoh's daughter, Shall I go and call to thee a nurse of the Hebrew women, that she may nurse the child for thee?*

*⁸ And Pharaoh's daughter said to her, Go. And the maid went and called the child's mother.*

*⁹ And Pharaoh's daughter said unto her, Take this child away, and nurse it for me, and I will give thee thy wages. And the*

*women took the child, and nursed it.*
*¹⁰And the child grew, and she brought him unto Pharaoh's daughter, and he became her son. And she called his name Moses: and she said, Because I drew him out of the water.*

*Exodus 2:5-10*

Jochebed, Moses' mother, a Hebrew woman, was employed to raise her own son in Pharaoh's palace at a time when Hebrew male children were being killed. This was no coincidence; it was part of God's *preparation plan* for Moses.

---

### *...whenever man tries to accomplish the will of God by his own carnal means it always backfires*

---

Moses grew up living in the best of both worlds. He was being educated in all the wisdom of the Egyptians *{Acts 7:22}* and, more importantly, his mother *{even though I am not sure he knew that was who she was}* was flooding his heart with *truth*. Jochebed would have introduced Moses to the God of Abraham, Isaac and Jacob; the God of the children of Israel. She would have told him continually about the wonderful things God had done for the children of Israel. She would have told him about God's promise to Abraham, Isaac and Jacob. Because she knew of these promises she would have believed that one day The Almighty God would deliver them from the bondage of the Egyptians. These words would not have escaped Moses' ears.

So, even though Moses was being raised as a *Prince of Egypt* he knew deep within that as long as the children of Israel were in bondage, so was he. Moses knew his roots, he was not confused. These Hebrew people in bondage, the children of Israel, were his people.

> $^{11}$*And it came to pass in those days, when Moses was grown, that he went out unto his brethren, and looked on their burdens: and he spied an Egyptian smiting an Hebrew, one of his BRETHREN.*

*Exodus 2:11*

It must have been this knowledge that pushed him into *taking the law into his own hands*. But, once again, we see that whenever man tries to accomplish the will of God by his own carnal means it ALWAYS backfires:

> $^{12}$*And he looked this way and that way, and when he saw that there was no man, he slew the Egyptian, and hid him in the sand.*
> $^{13}$*And when he went out the second day, behold, two men of the Hebrews strove together: and he said to him that did the wrong, Wherefore smitest thou thy fellow?*
> $^{14}$*And he said, Who made thee a prince and a judge over us? intendest thou to kill me, as thou killedst the Egyptian? And Moses feared, and said, Surely this thing is known.*
> $^{15}$*Now when Pharaoh heard this thing, he sought to slay Moses. But Moses fled from the face of Pharaoh, and dwelt in the land of Midian: and he sat down by a well.*

*Exodus 2:12-15*

In trying to help his brethren he became the enemy and had no choice but to run.

## The burning bush

Moses found himself in the land of Midian. He was introduced to Jethro the priest of Midian and found favour in his sight. Moses' heart was at rest in Midian and he ended up spending close to forty years in the land. During this time Moses lived in Jethro's house, married Zipporah, one of Jethro's seven daughters, had children and was also a faithful shepherd to Jethro's sheep. It was while Moses tended to his father-in-law's flock on Mount Sinai that he had his first recorded divine encounter.

*²And the angel of the LORD appeared unto him in a flame of fire out of the midst of a bush: and he looked, and, behold, the bush burned with fire, and the bush was not consumed. ³And Moses said, I WILL NOW TURN ASIDE, AND SEE THIS GREAT SIGHT, WHY THE BUSH IS NOT BURNT.*

*Exodus 3:2-3*

The *burning bush experience* marked the beginning of Moses' personal relationship with God and, once again, it was God Himself who initiated it. God presents Moses with a miraculous sight that he could not miss; *a burning bush that was not burning!* On seeing the bush Moses could have done a runner because this definitely was not a natural sight, but instead *he turned aside to take a look.* Moses saw the unburnt burning bush as *a great sight,* something supernatural. However, he did not know that it was the very presence of God. Even though Moses knew God *{he had heard about Him and things He had done}* he did not actually *know* Him *{he had not yet experienced God}.* But that was about to change.

In as much as Moses did not know that he was actually approaching the presence of God, and it seemed like this was all down to his curious sensitivity to the supernatural, the truth is that this was simply a *God incidence;* a divine set up. It is also interesting to note that it was only after Moses turned aside to take a look at the *unburnt* burning bush, only after he had taken a step in God's direction, that God actually called him, not a second earlier.

*⁴And when the LORD saw that he turned aside to see, God called unto him out of the midst of the bush, and said, Moses, Moses. And he said, Here am I.*
*⁵And he said, Draw not nigh hither: put off thy shoes from off thy feet, for the place whereon thou standest is holy ground.*
*⁶Moreover he said, I am the God of thy father, the God of Abraham, the God of Isaac, and the God of Jacob. And Moses*

*hid his face; for he was afraid to look upon God.*

*Exodus 3:4-6*

When Moses heard *the voice* from the burning bush he obeyed but he still did not know who was calling him. However, when God introduced Himself in *verse 6* the reality of the words spoken to him by Jochebed, his mother, back in Egypt would have struck a chord. Moses was overcome by reverential fear; the *second-hand relationship* he had with The Almighty God was about to become *real and personal.*

---

*...Moses had come to realise that all his inadequacies were insignificant simply because he now walked in the presence of Yahweh*

---

God had appeared to Abraham, Isaac and Jacob as *El-Elyon* and *'El Shaddai*; He had also appeared as *The Provider* and *The Shepherd*. But now He came to Moses as **I AM**; *I AM THAT I AM AND WHAT I AM AND WILL BE WHAT I WILL BE {Exodus 3:14}*. Moses would come to know God as **YAHWEH**, the One who depends on no one or nothing for His existence; the Limitless One, the one to whom nothing is impossible.

> [9]*Now therefore, behold, the cry of the children of Israel is come unto me: and I have also seen the oppression wherewith the Egyptians oppress them.*
> [10]*Come now therefore, and I will send thee unto Pharaoh, that thou mayest bring forth my people the children of Israel out of Egypt.*

*Exodus 3:9-10*

God, who had kept and prepared Moses and who also knew the burden He had placed in his heart, then revealed His plan; *Moses was to go back to Egypt and set the children of*

*Israel free.* Now, even though Moses had a burden for his enslaved Hebrew brethren, going back to Egypt would be like signing his own death warrant; *he was a fugitive!* Moses tried all he could to make God see that he was the *wrong person* for the job; *"...who am I?", "...when they ask for the name of He who sent me, what shall I say?", "...but they will not believe me or listen to and obey my voice...", "...I am not eloquent or a man of words,", "...I am slow of speech and have a heavy and awkward tongue" {Exodus 3:11 – Exodus 4:12}.* It was all in vain. Finally, Moses asked God to *please send someone else instead* but that was the last straw:

> ¹³And he said, O my LORD, send, I pray thee, by the hand of him whom thou wilt send.
> ¹⁴And the anger of the LORD was kindled against Moses, and he said, Is not Aaron the Levite thy brother? I know that he can speak well. And also, behold, he cometh forth to meet thee: and when he seeth thee, he will be glad in his heart.
>
> *Exodus 4:13-14*

God had promised that He would be with Moses, and Moses had come to realise *{albeit with a bit of persuading}* that all his inadequacies were insignificant simply because he now walked in the presence of Yahweh, **I AM THAT I AM.** Moses put his trust in God; he believed God and was ready to walk hand in hand with Him. It is amazing how, after Moses surrendered his heart to God, God told him that the thing he feared so much no longer existed:

> ¹⁹And the LORD said unto Moses in Midian, Go, return into Egypt: FOR ALL THE MEN ARE DEAD WHICH SOUGHT THY LIFE.
>
> *Exodus 4:19*

This, in a way, was no longer significant because Moses had already made a decision to walk in God's presence. But if God had told Moses this from the very beginning is it possible that Moses could have made a decision to return to Egypt based on the fact that he was a *free* man, thus placing little value on his trust in God?

## In His presence

Moses' walk in the presence of Yahweh was clear for all to see. After the struggle with the hard-hearted king of Egypt and finally shepherding the children of Israel *{approximately six hundred thousand men on foot, besides women and children}* out of the land, as God had promised in *Genesis 15:13-14*, the fruits of Moses' relationship with *The Limitless One* continued to abound.

Over and over again we see the hand of God move on behalf of the Israelites, and time and time again we see Moses step in on behalf of the children of Israel purely because of his relationship with Yahweh. From the pillar of cloud by day and the pillar of fire by night *{Exodus 13:21-22}*, to the parting of the Red Sea and the children of Israel walking through on dry ground *{Exodus 14:21-22}*, to the sweetening of the bitter waters of Marah *{Exodus 15:22-25}*, to the provision of manna in the wilderness *{Exodus 16:12-18, 35}*, to the water that miraculously flowed from the rock in Horeb *{Exodus 17:5-6}*, to the battle of Rephidim *{Exodus 17:8-14}*, to the Ten Commandments *{Exodus 20:1-17}*, and the Book of The Covenant *{Exodus 20:22 – 23:33 & Exodus 24:4}*, the list goes on. Exodus chapter 32 shines a bit more light on what God shared with Moses.

---

*...once again the power of relationship unlocked the mercy of God*

---

It was barely forty days after the children of Israel had agreed to do *ALL the words which the LORD hath said*

*{Exodus 24:3}*, barely forty nights after cutting a covenant with The Almighty God. The Israelites grew impatient with Moses' extended stay on Mount Sinai and word soon spread through the camp that maybe, just maybe, Moses would not come back. Not knowing what had become of Moses, or should we say not willing to wait for what God would tell them next through him, they gathered before Aaron and told him to make them gods. For some reason the promise they had made to God was no longer relevant. After all, the only man that God spoke to was gone, and they too needed *a god* that they could relate to.

> [8] *They have turned aside quickly out of the way which I commanded them: they have made them a molten calf, and have worshipped it, and have sacrificed thereunto, and said, These be thy gods, O Israel, which have brought thee up out of the land of Egypt.*
>
> *Exodus 32:8*

God, seeing that the children of Israel that Moses brought out of Egypt had already turned to worship a man-made golden calf, was ready to destroy them but...

> [9] *And the LORD said unto Moses, I have seen this people, and, behold, it is a stiffnecked people:*
>
> [10] *Now therefore let me alone, that my wrath may wax hot against them, and that I may consume them: and I will make of thee a great nation.*
>
> [11] *And Moses besought the LORD his God, and said, LORD, why doth thy wrath wax hot against thy people, which thou hast brought forth out of the land of Egypt with great power, and with a mighty hand?*
>
> [12] *Wherefore should the Egyptians speak, and say, For mischief did he bring them out, to slay them in the mountains, and to consume them from the face of the earth? Turn from thy fierce wrath, and repent of this evil against thy people.*
>
> [13] *Remember Abraham, Isaac, and Israel, thy servants, to whom thou swarest by thine own self, and saidst unto them, I will multiply your seed as the stars of heaven, and all this land that I have spoken of will I give unto your seed, and*

*they shall inherit it for ever.*

God asked Moses, a mere man who had chosen to trust in Him, to *let Him alone* so He could consume every one of these *stiff-necked people*. God even offered Moses an incentive by promising to make him a great nation. But Moses, knowing the heart of God and the promise God had made to Abraham, Isaac and Jacob, stood in the gap for the children of Israel and God showed His mercy.

> [14]*AND THE LORD REPENTED OF THE EVIL WHICH HE THOUGHT TO DO UNTO HIS PEOPLE.*

*Exodus 32:14*

---

## God spoke to Moses like a friend, face to face!

---

We see a similar situation in Exodus chapter 33 where God declares to Moses that He will remove His presence from the midst of the people *{verse 3}*. When Moses entered the Tabernacle the scriptures record that God's presence descended and He spoke to Moses *face to face, as a man speaketh unto his friend*. Here, once again, Moses entered into dialogue with The Almighty God and chose to stand in the gap for the children of Israel, and once again the power of relationship unlocked the mercy of God.

> [12]*And Moses said unto the LORD, See, thou sayest unto me, Bring up this people: and thou hast not let me know whom thou wilt send with me. Yet thou hast said, I know thee by name, and thou hast also found grace in my sight.*
> [13]*Now therefore, I pray thee, if I have found grace in thy sight, shew me now thy way, that I may know thee, that I may find grace in thy sight: and consider that this nation is thy people.*
> [14]*And he said, MY PRESENCE SHALL GO WITH THEE, AND I WILL GIVE THEE REST.*

But it did not end there. When Moses says, *"I beseech thee, shew me Thy glory" {verse 18}* you almost get the feeling that he is about to be struck down but alas...

> [19]*And he said, I will make all my goodness pass before thee, and I will proclaim the name of the LORD before thee; and will be gracious to whom I will be gracious, and will shew mercy on whom I will shew mercy.*
> [20]*And he said, Thou canst not see my face: for there shall no man see me, and live.*
> [21]*And the LORD said, Behold, there is a place by me, and thou shalt stand upon a rock:*
> [22]*And it shall come to pass, while my glory passeth by, that I will put thee in a clift of the rock, and will cover thee with my hand while I pass by:*
> [23]*And I will take away mine hand, and thou shalt see my back parts: but my face shall not be seen.*

*Exodus 33:19-23*

Now, if that is not mind blowing then what is? To cap it all, even though Moses did not enter the Promised Land *{because of the incident at the waters of MeribahKadesh}* he was the first person recorded in scripture that God actually showed ALL the land that He promised to Abraham, Isaac and Jacob; the land flowing with milk and honey:

> [1]*And Moses went up from the plains of Moab unto the mountain of Nebo, to the top of Pisgah, that is over against Jericho. AND THE LORD SHEWED HIM ALL THE LAND of Gilead, unto Dan,*
> [2]*And all Naphtali, and the land of Ephraim, and Manasseh, and all the land of Judah, unto the utmost sea,*
> [3]*And the south, and the plain of the valley of Jericho, the city of palm trees, unto Zoar.*
> [4]*And the LORD said unto him, THIS IS THE LAND WHICH I SWARE UNTO ABRAHAM, UNTO ISAAC, AND UNTO JACOB, SAYING, I WILL GIVE IT UNTO THY SEED: I HAVE CAUSED THEE TO SEE IT WITH THINE EYES, BUT THOU SHALT NOT*

*Deuteronomy 34:1-4*

Moses was special. He received his inspiration and direction from God. When no one believed he believed. When God's chosen people turned their backs on God, Moses stood in the gap; he was *the believing mediator.* However, Moses was only able to stand firm because he continually fellowshipped with Yahweh. Because he lived in the presence of God he grew to know the heart of God. The relationship Moses shared with The Limitless One was not one that needed a "middle-man"; it was real and it was personal. God spoke to Moses on a one to one basis; God spoke to Moses like a friend, *face to face!*

> [11]*And THE LORD SPAKE UNTO MOSES FACE TO FACE, AS A MAN SPEAKETH UNTO HIS FRIEND. And he turned again into the camp: but his servant Joshua, the son of Nun, a young man, departed not out of the tabernacle.*

*Exodus 33:11*

> [10]*And there arose not a prophet since in Israel like unto Moses, WHOM THE LORD KNEW FACE TO FACE,*

*Deuteronomy 34:10*

# A MAN AFTER GOD'S HEART

The Lord had sent Samuel to anoint Saul as the first king of Israel. The scriptures describe Saul as one of a kind; *there was not among the children of Israel a goodlier person than he: from his shoulders and upward he was higher than any of the people {1 Samuel 9:2}.* We also see that Saul was a humble man *{1 Samuel 9:21}.* But then he was faced with the *Amalek assignment.*

King Saul was told to *smite Amalek,* and **utterly destroy** *all that they have, and spare them not {I Samuel 15:3}.* After hearing the word of the Lord, King Saul gathered his troops, went into the city of Amalek and *utterly destroyed all the Amalekites with the edge of the sword.* However, Saul somehow *"forgot"* to kill *Agag, king of the Amalekites, and the best of the sheep, oxen, fatlings and the lambs {I Samuel 15:9}.* Seeing that Saul had turned from following Him, and had not performed His commandments, God sent Samuel to tell Saul that in His sight he was no longer the king of Israel.

> [26]*And Samuel said unto Saul, I will not return with thee: for thou hast rejected the word of the LORD, and the LORD hath*

*rejected thee from being king over Israel.*

*²⁷And as Samuel turned about to go away, he laid hold upon the skirt of his mantle, and it rent.*

*²⁸And Samuel said unto him, THE LORD HATH RENT THE KINGDOM OF ISRAEL FROM THEE THIS DAY, AND HATH GIVEN IT TO A NEIGHBOUR OF THINE, THAT IS BETTER THAN THOU.*

*I Samuel 15:26-28*

This act of disobedience spiritually marked *the end* of Saul's reign over Israel. But who was this *neighbour* that God intended to hand the Kingdom of Israel to?

## The chosen one

After rebuking Samuel for continually mourning Saul's rejection, God tells him to arise and go to the house of Jesse the Bethlehemite; God had chosen one of Jesse's eight sons to be the next king of Israel. Samuel was a bit reluctant because he knew if Saul heard about this mission it could mean the end of his life. But, as usual, God had a plan:

*²And Samuel said, How can I go? if Saul hear it, he will kill me. And the LORD said, Take an heifer with thee, and say, I am come to sacrifice to the LORD.*

*³And call Jesse to the sacrifice, and I will shew thee what thou shalt do: and thou shalt anoint unto me him whom I name unto thee.*

*1 Samuel 16:2-3*

After consecrating Jesse and his sons, Samuel called them to join him in worshipping God. The time had come to anoint the next king of Israel. One look at Eliab, Jesse's firstborn, and Samuel was sure that he had spotted the Lord's anointed. But even though Eliab seemed to have the looks and stature of a king, he was not God's chosen one.

*⁷But the LORD said unto Samuel, Look not on his countenance, or on the height of his stature; because I have refused him: for the LORD seeth not as man seeth; for man looketh on the outward appearance, but the LORD looketh on the heart.*

*1 Samuel 16:7*

Samuel now knew what God was looking for and as the last of the seven sons that Jesse had presented passed before Samuel it soon became clear that *the chosen one* was not among them. So, where was he?

*[11]And Samuel said unto Jesse, Are here all thy children? And he said, There remaineth yet the youngest, and, behold, he keepeth the sheep. And Samuel said unto Jesse, Send and fetch him: for we will not sit down till he come hither.*

*1 Samuel 16:11*

## *David was the chosen one; the anointed king of Israel*

Jesse did not consider including David in the line up because it most likely did not cross his mind. Even though he was bright-eyed and good-looking, David was more of a runt than a hunk. You also get the impression that he was looked down upon by the others; after all you cannot exactly compare tending sheep to being in the mighty Israeli army. If only they knew what he got up to while looking after those sheep then maybe their opinion of him might have been a little different. Well, at the end of the day God always looks at the heart.

When David finally arrived God told Samuel to *arise and anoint him*. Samuel anointed David in the presence of his brothers *{I wonder what was going through their minds?}* and as he did the Spirit of the Lord came upon David.

*[13]Then Samuel took the horn of oil, and anointed him in the midst of his brethren: and the Spirit of the LORD came upon*

*David from that day forward. So Samuel rose up, and went to Ramah.*

*1 Samuel 16:13*

David was the chosen one; *the anointed king of Israel.* But, as David would soon find out, it was a long way to the throne.

## The journey to the palace

Even though Saul was still the king of Israel the presence of God had left him. When the Spirit of God departed from Saul a spirit of depression settled on him. Saul's servants noticed that the king was not himself and asked if they could help. Their suggestion was to find a skilful harp player that would play and lift the king whenever he was depressed. Saul agreed to their suggestion and asked them to find that *special someone.* In stepped David.

> [18] *Then answered one of the servants, and said, Behold, I have seen a son of Jesse the Bethlehemite, that is cunning in playing, and a mighty valiant man, and a man of war, and prudent in matters, and a comely person, and the LORD is with him.*
>
> [19] *Wherefore Saul sent messengers unto Jesse, and said, Send me David thy son, which is with the sheep.*
>
> [20] *And Jesse took an ass laden with bread, and a bottle of wine, and a kid, and sent them by David his son unto Saul.*
>
> [21] *And David came to Saul, and stood before him: and he loved him greatly; and he became his armourbearer.*
>
> [22] *And Saul sent to Jesse, saying, Let David, I pray thee, stand before me; for he hath found favour in my sight.*
>
> [23] *And it came to pass, when the evil spirit from God was upon Saul, that David took an harp, and played with his hand: so Saul was refreshed, and was well, and the evil spirit departed from him.*

*1 Samuel 16:18-23*

This was the first mention of David after he had been anointed and he is described by one of Saul's servants as an excellent musician, a valiant man, a man of war, an attractive person, prudent in speech and eloquent; and to cap it all, "the Lord is with him". I thought David was just a shepherd boy? Suddenly he was being described as a courageous man of war, and he was not even in Saul's army. *That is what happens when the presence of God fills a life!*

David's God-given gift of music opened the door to the palace and brought him before King Saul. When he stood before Saul he found immediate favour in his sight. In a twinkle of an eye David had a free pass into the palace and had become the king's personal musician. Saul also made David one of his armour-bearers. An armour-bearer was usually selected because of his bravery, not only to bear armour, but also to stand by the king in time of danger. Even though David was not a member of the Israeli army Saul somehow trusted him enough to place him in this position. *That is what happens when the presence of God fills a life!*

## The valley of Elah
Almost everyone knows the story of David and Goliath so I will try not to bore you with the details but as David prepares to take out this uncircumcised philistine we come to see a few things.

David found himself on the battle field because his father had asked him to take food to his brothers Eliab, Abinadab and Shammah; they were soldiers in Saul's army. It was while he was greeting his brothers that Goliath stepped forward and issued his *one on one, winner takes all challenge.* But when the men of Israel saw Goliath they were afraid and ran away. Apparently Goliath had been taunting the Israeli army in this manner for a while, about forty days. But the one thing that made today different was that

David, *a young man filled with the Spirit of God*, heard. This situation did not go down well with David and he did not hesitate to express this:

> <sup>26</sup>*And David spake to the men that stood by him, saying, What shall be done to the man that killeth this Philistine, and taketh away the reproach from Israel? for who is this uncircumcised Philistine, that he should defy the armies of the living God?*

> *1 Samuel 17:26*

---

## Killing Goliath really deserved no reward because this situation should not have presented itself in the first place

---

It has been said that David was motivated by the *prize* i.e. a huge reward, the king's daughter and the freedom of *his father's house,* but I tend to disagree. In fact taking a closer look we see that first of all, it is not recorded that David ever received this huge reward. Secondly, Saul promised David his eldest daughter Merab, but that did not happen {*1 Samuel 18:17,19},* and if not for Saul's evil motive I doubt if David would have ever become Saul's son-in-law. And thirdly, the scriptures are silent on Jesse's household being tax exempt; most likely that did not happen either. I believe the primary reason why David asked about the reward was because he was actually trying to find out the worth that had been placed on getting rid of someone who was worth little or nothing in God's sight.

Note that David called Goliath *an uncircumcised philistine*. To the children of Israel circumcision was the sign of God's covenant protection. First of all Goliath was uncircumcised and therefore did not qualify for divine protection, and secondly he was a philistine who worshiped a dead god. To David, Goliath belonged to the army of a dead god and therefore had no protection, so where did he get off challenging the army of the Living God? Killing Goliath really deserved no reward because this situation should not have presented itself in the first place.

Finally, David's words reach Saul and he is ushered into the king's presence. David reveals that he is willing to take on Goliath. Saul brings up the issue of David's lack of warfare experience and that is when David lets the king in on his little secret:

> <sup>34</sup>And David said unto Saul, Thy servant kept his father's sheep, and there came a lion, and a bear, and took a lamb out of the flock:
> <sup>35</sup>And I went out after him, and smote him, and delivered it out of his mouth: and when he arose against me, I caught him by his beard, and smote him, and slew him.
> <sup>36</sup>Thy servant slew both the lion and the bear: and this uncircumcised Philistine shall be as one of them, seeing he hath defied the armies of the living God.
> <sup>37</sup>David said moreover, The LORD that delivered me out of the paw of the lion, and out of the paw of the bear, he will deliver me out of the hand of this Philistine. And Saul said unto David, Go, and the LORD be with thee.

> 1 Samuel 17:34-37

Even though David was *just* a shepherd boy he had experienced things that Saul's soldiers could only dream of; he had slain a lion and killed a bear. But more importantly David knew that the slaying of these animals was definitely not by his own power; he knew that *it was the LORD that had delivered him out of the claw of the lion and the paw of the bear*. David's trust was in the Lord. David knew beyond a shadow of a doubt that he would overcome. He believed that the living God would deliver him from this uncircumcised philistine.

After making a believer out of Saul and picking the armour and weapons of his choice *{a staff, five smooth stones, a shepherd's bag and a sling}*, David went out to meet Goliath. When Goliath finally noticed David he could not help but think that this was some kind of joke; the Israeli army had forty days to come up with a champion and all they could offer was a boy with a stick in his hand. Goliath promised *to give David's flesh to the birds of the air and the beasts of the field* but listen to David's response:

> <sup>45</sup> *Then said David to the Philistine, Thou comest to me with a sword, and with a spear, and with a shield: but I come to thee in the name of the LORD of hosts, the God of the armies of Israel, whom thou hast defied.*
>
> <sup>46</sup> *This day will the LORD deliver thee into mine hand; and I will smite thee, and take thine head from thee; and I will give the carcases of the host of the Philistines this day unto the fowls of the air, and to the wild beasts of the earth; that all the earth may know that there is a God in Israel.*
>
> <sup>47</sup> *And all this assembly shall know that the LORD saveth not with sword and spear: for the battle is the LORD's, and he will give you into our hands.*
>
> 1 Samuel 17:45-47

Goliath came to David with natural weapons *{a sword, a spear and a shield}* but David approached him with a supernatural weapon: **the name of the Lord of hosts.** David's words were not empty; they were spoken from a heart of relationship. Though young, David knew that God was his shepherd. He believed that God would never leave nor forsake him, and that he was safe under the shadow of His wings. It was this understanding that David had when he, as a shepherd boy, killed the lion and the bear that had tried to steal a lamb from his flock. It was this same understanding he had as he stood before Goliath.

This battle had nothing to do with warfare experience,

weapons and size; it was a battle between a giant who had an impersonal relationship with a dead god and a lad who had a personal relationship with the One True God. Even though David killed Goliath with a sling and a stone I believe he could have slain Goliath by simply throwing a piece of paper with his bare hands. Goliath did not stand a chance because the battle was not against David; it was against the one David had a relationship with: *the Lord of hosts.*

After the battle in the valley of Elah David became a prominent figure in Saul's palace. He was made a Commander in Saul's army and was respected by Saul's servants and all the people of Israel. But the more the people loved David the more Saul hated him. Saul tried several times to kill David but to no avail *{1 Samuel* **18***:11,17-21;* **19***:1,10-11,20,31;* **23***:7-8,14,23-26}.* When David had a chance to smite Saul he knew that touching the Lord's anointed was not a wise idea. At the end of the day even Saul had to acknowledge that truly **the Lord was with David.**

---

*The fellowship that David shared with God created a special place for David in God's heart*

---

## A heart relationship

David may not have been *Mr Perfect* but he had the right heart. All through his lifetime, before and after he became the king of Israel until the day he died, we see that he had a heart relationship with God. The fellowship that David shared with God created a special place for David in God's heart. It was out of this personal relationship that David had an understanding of God and His ways. This understanding shows up all through David's life; when he killed the lion, when he slaughtered the bear, when he took out Goliath, even when he spared Saul.

From the time God delivered Goliath into David's hands, David found favour in the sight of Israel and, even though he was still king, Saul gradually faded into the background. This whole episode had an adverse effect on Saul's relationship with David. In fact things got so bad that it seemed like the only reason Saul existed was to kill David. You would therefore expect that if David's number one enemy fell into his hands David would not hesitate to do the *necessary*; after all, he was God's chosen one and if he did not put an end to Saul's life he would always be on the run. So you can imagine what was going through the minds of David's men the first time Saul fell into their hands.

Saul had gathered three thousand of his troops and was once again after David. In the midst of his search Saul went into a cave to relieve himself. This happened to be the cave David and his men were hiding in. David's men could not believe their good fortune. They were hiding from the enemy and suddenly the fate of the enemy was in their hands. Thinking this could only be the hand of God, David's men encouraged him to end this once and for all. So, David arose, crept over to Saul and cut off a piece of the king's royal robe. But immediately he did this he knew he was in the wrong:

> *⁶And he said unto his men, THE LORD FORBID THAT I SHOULD DO THIS THING UNTO MY MASTER, THE LORD'S ANOINTED, TO STRETCH FORTH MINE HAND AGAINST HIM, SEEING HE IS THE ANOINTED OF THE LORD.*
> *⁷So David stayed his servants with these words, and suffered them not to rise against Saul. But Saul rose up out of the cave, and went on his way.*
> *⁸David also arose afterward, and went out of the cave, and*

*cried after Saul, saying, My lord the king. And when Saul looked behind him, David stooped with his face to the earth, and bowed himself.*

<sup></sup>*¹⁰Behold, this day thine eyes have seen how that the LORD had delivered thee to day into mine hand in the cave: and some bade me kill thee: but mine eye spared thee; and I said, I WILL NOT PUT FORTH MINE HAND AGAINST MY LORD; FOR HE IS THE LORD'S ANOINTED.*

*¹²The LORD judge between me and thee, and the LORD avenge me of thee: but mine hand shall not be upon thee.*

*1 Samuel 24:6-8,10,12*

Even after Saul seemingly repented of his wicked ways we are presented with a similar situation in 1 Samuel chapter 26. Once again Saul and three thousand troops were on David's trail after being tipped off by the Ziphites, and once again David is faced with an opportunity to kill Saul, this time inside Saul's tent. But once again, to Abishai's surprise, David chooses not to take advantage of the situation:

*⁸Then said Abishai to David, God hath delivered thine enemy into thine hand this day: now therefore let me smite him, I pray thee, with the spear even to the earth at once, and I will not smite him the second time.*

*⁹And David said to Abishai, Destroy him not: FOR WHO CAN STRETCH FORTH HIS HAND AGAINST THE LORD'S ANOINTED, AND BE GUILTLESS?*

*¹⁰David said furthermore, AS THE LORD LIVETH, THE LORD SHALL SMITE HIM; or his day shall come to die; or he shall descend into battle, and perish.*

*1 Samuel 26:8-10*

---

*David found peace and refuge in God and knew that as long as he stayed in His presence he was safe.*

---

Though God had rejected Saul, David knew that Saul had been appointed by God. Even though David knew that God had chosen him as the next king of Israel he also knew that when God wanted Saul off the throne, He would do it His way. David understood that if anyone was going to smite Saul it would be The One who anointed Saul. David found peace and refuge in God and knew that as long as he stayed in His presence he was safe. *Maybe if Saul understood this it might have made sense to him why, no matter how hard he tried, David kept slipping out of his hands.* David knew the heart of God because God held a special place in his heart.

## Intimacy

The depth of David's relationship with God was phenomenal. Because of the intimacy that existed in their relationship David knew he could speak to God with an assurance that God would speak to him. David also understood that God knew the end from the beginning and was able to turn around *the impossible.* As long as David heard from God he knew he could not go wrong so it comes as no surprise that David constantly asked God for wisdom to handle situations.

---

### *David enquired of the Lord habitually*

---

When David wanted to know if he should smite the Philistines that were fighting against Keilah, and robbing the threshing floors, he enquired of the LORD {1 Samuel 23:1-2}. When David wanted to know if the men of Keilah would deliver him into Saul's hands, he enquired of the LORD {1 Samuel 23:10-11}. When David wanted to know if he should pursue the Amalekites that captured their wives, sons and daughters, he enquired of the LORD {1 Samuel 30:8}. When David was not sure if he should go up into any of the cities of Judah, he enquired of the LORD {2

Samuel 2:1}. David enquired of the Lord habitually. Each time he did he knew that God would tell him what to do. Each time he obeyed the divine instruction he knew that victory was certain. David knew this because what he shared with God was real and personal.

It is also important to note that David did not take his relationship with God for granted. We see an example of this when the philistines planned to fight David and his army in the valley of Rephaim {2 Samuel 5:17-21}. David asks if he should go up and fight the Philistines and God tells him to go ahead for He will surely deliver the Philistines into David's hand {vs19}. Interestingly, the exact situation presents itself when, after being defeated, the stubborn philistines deployed their troops in valley of Rephaim again. David could have assumed this was a similar situation so most likely there was no need to enquire of the Lord, as God's response would most likely be the same. But check this out:

> [23]And when David enquired of the LORD, he said, THOU SHALT NOT GO UP; but fetch a compass behind them, and come upon them over against the mulberry trees.
> [24]And let it be, when thou hearest the sound of a going in the tops of the mulberry trees, that then thou shalt bestir thyself: for then shall the LORD go out before thee, to smite the host of the Philistines.
> [25]And David did so, as the LORD had commanded him; and smote the Philistines from Geba until thou come to Gazer.
>
> *2 Samuel 5:23-25*

Truly, God's thoughts are not our thoughts and our ways not His ways {Isaiah 55:8-9}. David knew that though the circumstances seemed the same there was a need to find out what God would have him do. This was something he had learnt by spending time in the presence of God.

## A heart for God

As mentioned earlier, David may not have been the perfect man but he definitely had a heart for God. That explains why each time his imperfections popped up, rather than hide from God, he ran into God. Take the *Bathsheba incident* in 2 Samuel chapters 11 and 12.

David decides to stay home when really he should have been at war. He goes for a stroll on the roof top and sees this beauty having a bath. David asks who she is and is told that she is Bathsheba, the wife of Uriah, a Hittite soldier in his army. The rest is history; David sleeps with Bathsheba, she gets pregnant, David tries to cover things up and when that goes wrong he ends up *killing* Uriah.

So, God sent Nathan to David with the Parable of the rich man and the poor man. The second Nathan likens David to the rich man in the parable we immediately see, from David's response, where David's heart is:

> [13]*And David said unto Nathan, I HAVE SINNED AGAINST THE LORD. And Nathan said unto David, The LORD also hath put away thy sin; thou shalt not die.*
>
> 2 Samuel 12:13

It was after this incident that David wrote Psalms 32 & 51; Psalms focussed solely on David expressing a heart of forgiveness to God. David knew he had sinned against God and repentantly falls at His feet. Even in the midst of such a great sin David still hides in God.

> [1]*Blessed is he whose transgression is forgiven, whose sin is covered.*
> [2]*Blessed is the man unto whom the LORD imputeth not iniquity, and in whose spirit there is no guile.*
> [3]*When I kept silence, my bones waxed old through my roaring all the day long.*
> [4]*For day and night thy hand was heavy upon me: my moisture*

*is turned into the drought of summer. Selah.*

⁵*I ACKNOWLEDGE MY SIN UNTO THEE, AND MINE INIQUITY HAVE I NOT HID. I SAID, I WILL CONFESS MY TRANSGRESSIONS UNTO THE LORD; AND THOU FORGAVEST THE INIQUITY OF MY SIN. Selah.*

⁶*For this shall every one that is godly pray unto thee in a time when thou mayest be found: surely in the floods of great waters they shall not come nigh unto him.*

⁷*THOU ART MY HIDING PLACE; THOU SHALT PRESERVE ME FROM TROUBLE; thou shalt compass me about with songs of deliverance. Selah.*

¹⁰*MANY SORROWS SHALL BE TO THE WICKED: BUT HE THAT TRUSTETH IN THE LORD, MERCY SHALL COMPASS HIM ABOUT.*

*Psalm 32:1-7, 10*

¹*HAVE MERCY UPON ME, O GOD, ACCORDING TO THY LOVINGKINDNESS: ACCORDING UNTO THE MULTITUDE OF THY TENDER MERCIES BLOT OUT MY TRANSGRESSIONS.*

²*Wash me throughly from mine iniquity, and cleanse me from my sin.*

³*For I acknowledge my transgressions: and my sin is ever before me.*

¹⁰*CREATE IN ME A CLEAN HEART, O GOD; AND RENEW A RIGHT SPIRIT WITHIN ME.*

¹¹*CAST ME NOT AWAY FROM THY PRESENCE; AND TAKE NOT THY HOLY SPIRIT FROM ME.*

¹²*RESTORE UNTO ME THE JOY OF THY SALVATION; AND UPHOLD ME WITH THY FREE SPIRIT.*

¹³*Then will I teach transgressors thy ways; and sinners shall be converted unto thee.*

¹⁴*Deliver me from bloodguiltiness, O God, thou God of my salvation: and my tongue shall sing aloud of thy righteousness.*

¹⁵*O Lord, open thou my lips; and my mouth shall shew forth thy praise.*

¹⁶*FOR THOU DESIREST NOT SACRIFICE; ELSE WOULD I GIVE IT: THOU DELIGHTEST NOT IN BURNT OFFERING.*

¹⁷*THE SACRIFICES OF GOD ARE A BROKEN SPIRIT: A BROKEN AND A CONTRITE HEART, O GOD, THOU WILT NOT DESPISE.*

*Psalm 51:1-3, 10-17*

Then there was the time when David decided to take a census of Israel. Immediately after completing the census the scriptures make us realise that David knew he had wronged God. Realising he had acted foolishly he asks for forgiveness; he runs into God.

> [10]*And David's heart smote him after that he had numbered the people. And David said unto the LORD, I have sinned greatly in that I have done: and now, I BESEECH THEE, O LORD, TAKE AWAY THE INIQUITY OF THY SERVANT; FOR I HAVE DONE VERY FOOLISHLY.*
>
> [14]*And David said unto Gad, I am in a great strait: LET US FALL NOW INTO THE HAND OF THE LORD; FOR HIS MERCIES ARE GREAT: and let me not fall into the hand of man.*
>
> *2 Samuel 24:10,14*

## *Giving God heartfelt worship was David's number one priority*

David's willingness to fall into the hands of God rather than the hands of man says it all. David knew that God was merciful; he had been the recipient of this mercy time and time again. David was sure he could depend on God's mercy, but he could not say the same for man. He could, in a sense, vouch for God because he knew God.

Over the years David's trust and love for God grew immensely. David had come to know God as his shepherd, his rock, his fortress, his refuge, his buckler, his salvation, his deliverer, his strength and his strong tower. And when David pours out his heart in Psalms chapters 18 and 23 we get to have a taste of what the relationship he shared with God actually meant to him. David acknowledged from his heart that everything he was came down to the fact that his life was hidden in God.

Giving God heartfelt worship was David's number one priority. David loved God, he loved His word, he loved to fellowship with God, he delighted in offering praise and thanksgiving to God and David did not hesitate to do the will of God. David had a heart for God so when God calls him a man after His heart it somehow comes as no surprise.

> [14]But now thy kingdom shall not continue: THE LORD HATH SOUGHT HIM A MAN AFTER HIS OWN HEART, and the LORD hath commanded him to be captain over his people, because thou hast not kept that which the LORD commanded thee.
>
> *1 Samuel 13:14*

> [22]And when he had removed him, he raised up unto them David to be their king; to whom also he gave their testimony, and said, I have found David the son of Jesse, a man after mine own heart, which shall fulfil all my will.
>
> *Acts 13:22*

# THE WORD BECAME FLESH

I t may seem a little strange to look at the relationship between God the Father and God the Son. After all, they are one so it is only natural for *their* relationship to be perfect. But, inasmuch as this is true I believe that it is no coincidence that *the Word became flesh, and dwelt among us.* The truth is that though Jesus was all God, He was also *all man*.

## "All man"

Jesus was *all* God, but when He chose to drop His divine cloak and walk the earth as a man He took on the limitations of mankind. We are made to realise that, just like us, Jesus grew in wisdom and favour with God and man *{Luke 2:52}*. If Jesus had come as God the need for wisdom and favour would have been irrelevant simply because God is *wisdom and favour personified*. Jesus walked the earth as all man.

As a man, Jesus was tempted in every imaginable way but He never fell for a temptation. Jesus went through everything we go through and He is familiar with every mountain and valley we face along this *human pathway*. We therefore have an assurance that Jesus is not a stranger to the issues we face. We can actually go to our merciful and faithful High Priest *{Hebrews 2:16-18}* in confidence and without fear knowing that we can receive mercy and find grace in our time of need. We can go to Jesus knowing that He understands.

> *[14] Seeing then that we have a great high priest, that is passed into the heavens, Jesus the Son of God, let us hold fast our profession.*
> *[15] For we have not an high priest which cannot be touched with the feeling of our infirmities; but was in all points tempted like as we are, yet without sin.*
> *[16] Let us therefore come boldly unto the throne of grace, that we may obtain mercy, and find grace to help in time of need.*
>
> Hebrews 4:14-16

---

*He stood where we stand, walked where we walk, and felt what we feel. Jesus walked the earth as all man*

---

Jesus had His fair share of every human feeling and emotion. He **wept** *{Luke 19:41-42; John 11:35}* and **slept** *{Mark 4:37-38}*, He **hungered** *{Matthew 4:2; Mark 11:12}* and **thirsted** *{John 4:7}*. Jesus knew what it was like to feel **tired** *{John 4:6}* and He definitely knew what it felt like to **toil**; remember he was not just a carpenter's son, He himself was a carpenter *{Mark 6:3}*. Jesus experienced **distress** and **sorrow** *{Matthew 26:36-38}*, **anger** *{John 2:14-16; Mark 3:5}* and **disappointment** *{Mark 14:37-38}* and it goes without saying that He knew what it was like to feel **compassion** *{Mark 6:34; Mark 8:2; Matthew 14:14; Matthew 20:34; Mark 1:40-41; Luke 7:12-13; John 11:33; the compassion list goes on and on!}*. Name it, Jesus tasted it. He stood where we stand, walked where we walk, and felt what we feel. Jesus walked the earth as *all man.*

## Evidence of The Presence

For about thirty years Jesus' life was mainly kept under wraps. After His birth the scriptures record that Jesus grew; *He became strong in spirit and was filled with wisdom.* However, more importantly, *the grace of God was upon Him.* At the age of twelve Jesus went on the customary trip to Jerusalem with His parents for the Passover feast. Unknown to Mary and Joseph Jesus decided to stay behind after the feast. When it finally dawned on them that Jesus was actually missing their search began. On the third day they found Him:

> [46] *And it came to pass, that after three days they found him in the temple, sitting in the midst of the doctors, both hearing them, and asking them questions.*
> [47] *And all that heard him were astonished at his understanding and answers.*
> [48] *And when they saw him, they were amazed: and his mother said unto him, Son, why hast thou thus dealt with us? behold, thy father and I have sought thee sorrowing.*
> [49] *And he said unto them, How is it that ye sought me? WIST YE NOT THAT I MUST BE ABOUT MY FATHER'S BUSINESS?*
>
> Luke 2:46-49

At the age of twelve Jesus is said to have an extraordinary understanding of the scriptures. He was sitting in the presence of teachers of the word and demonstrating wisdom far beyond his years, *and I dare say far above the intelligence of the teachers.* We also see Jesus mention *His Father's business;* something that confused Mary and Joseph. We must not fail to realise that Jesus' mesmerising wisdom and the understanding He had of His Father's business at the tender age of twelve were evidence that the boy Jesus experienced the presence of The Father.

## The Father's will

At about the age of thirty Jesus steps out and turns the world upside down as we witness various manifestations of His *Father's business*. For approximately three years miracles followed Him everywhere He went; signs and wonders that blew away the mindsets of men. The people could not comprehend Him and, even though they turned against Him, somewhere in the back of their minds they knew there was something really special about this carpenter from Bethlehem. What they did not understand was that *special something* actually had its roots in the intimate relationship Jesus shared with His Father.

---

*Jesus naturally knew His Father's heart because He permanently dwelt in His Father's presence*

---

Throughout the New Testament we see that Jesus went about His Father's business with a passion. Jesus lived to do His Father's business; He lived to carry out the will of His Father. Jesus walked the earth with one purpose: **To please His Father.** Jesus lived to put a smile on His Father's face.

> [34]*Jesus saith unto them, MY MEAT IS TO DO THE WILL OF HIM THAT SENT ME, and to finish his work.*
>
> *John 4:34*

> [38]*For I came down from heaven, NOT TO DO MINE OWN WILL, BUT THE WILL OF HIM THAT SENT ME.*
>
> *John 6:38*

> [29]*And he that sent me is with me: the Father hath not left me alone; FOR I DO ALWAYS THOSE THINGS THAT PLEASE HIM.*
>
> *John 8:29*

> [41]*And he was withdrawn from them about a stone's cast, and*

*kneeled down, and prayed,*
*⁴²Saying, Father, if thou be willing, remove this cup from me: NEVERTHELESS NOT MY WILL, BUT THINE, BE DONE.*

*Luke 22:41-42*

Jesus subjected Himself to the Father's will, even at those times when it was least convenient. Everything He did and said came from The Father. He did what the Father showed Him to do, and spoke what His Father told Him to speak:

*¹⁹Then answered Jesus and said unto them, Verily, verily, I say unto you, The Son can do nothing of himself, but what he seeth the Father do: for what things soever he doeth, these also doeth the Son likewise.*
*²⁰For the Father loveth the Son, and sheweth him all things that himself doeth: and he will shew him greater works than these, that ye may marvel.*

*John 5:19-20*

*²⁸Then said Jesus unto them, When ye have lifted up the Son of man, then shall ye know that I am he, and that I do nothing of myself; but as my Father hath taught me, I speak these things.*

*John 8:28*

*⁴⁹For I have not spoken of myself; but the Father which sent me, he gave me a commandment, what I should say, and what I should speak.*
*⁵⁰And I know that his commandment is life everlasting: whatsoever I speak therefore, even as the Father said unto me, so I speak.*

*John 12:49-50*

Because Jesus did the will of The Father there was a manifestation of The Father's power everywhere He went. Jesus knew The Father's will because of the genuine relationship that existed between them. Jesus naturally knew His Father's heart because He permanently dwelt in His Father's presence.

# Hand in hand

We see from scripture that the man Jesus walked hand in hand with God the Father. Jesus did NOTHING without His Father's approval. Because Jesus lived in the presence of God doing God's will came to Him naturally. When Jesus spoke He knew He was speaking The Father's will because His life was totally submitted to Him. When Jesus did anything He had no doubts that He was doing the will of His Father because He was obediently carrying out what The Father had told Him. Jesus lived, walked and carried around His Father's presence. He lived in His Father and His Father lived in Him, and because of this depth of intimacy *THEY WERE ONE.*

> *[21]That they all may be one; AS THOU, FATHER, ART IN ME, AND I IN THEE, that they also may be one in us: that the world may believe that thou hast sent me.*
> *[22]And the glory which thou gavest me I have given them; that they may be one, EVEN AS WE ARE ONE:*
>
> *John 17:21-22*
>
> *[30]I AND THE FATHER ARE ONE.*
>
> *John 10:30*

It is impossible to go through The Gospels without seeing evidence of Jesus' intimacy with The Father. Be it when He went away to pray, when He spent time with His disciples or even when He was in the midst of the multitude, Jesus carried around the very presence of God the Father.

Jesus was constantly speaking with, to and about His Father. When He slipped away to pray...

> *[12]And it came to pass in those days, that he went out into a mountain to pray, and continued all night in prayer to God.*
>
> *Luke 6:12*
>
> *[35]And in the morning, rising up a great while before day,*

*he went out, and departed into a solitary place, and there prayed.*

*Mark 1:35*

[16]*And he withdrew himself into the wilderness, and prayed.*

*Luke 5:16*

When He was in the presence of His disciples *{John chapter 17}*, and when He was in the midst of the people...

[41]*Then they took away the stone from the place where the dead was laid. And Jesus lifted up his eyes, and said, Father, I THANK THEE THAT THOU HAST HEARD ME.*
[42]*AND I KNEW THAT THOU HEAREST ME ALWAYS: BUT BECAUSE OF THE PEOPLE WHICH STAND BY I SAID IT, THAT THEY MAY BELIEVE THAT THOU HAST SENT ME.*

*John 11:41-42*

[28]*FATHER, GLORIFY THY NAME. Then came there a voice from heaven, saying, I have both glorified it, and will glorify it again.*
[29]*The people therefore, that stood by, and heard it, said that it thundered: others said, An angel spake to him.*

*John 12:28-29*

Even Jesus' parables focussed primarily on The Father and The Kingdom. Jesus' whereabouts or the nature of the people He was with did not hinder His relationship with The Father in any way. Jesus always spoke from His heart, and the content of His heart was The Father's will.

---

*When the first Adam fell divine relationship was broken, but when the last Adam rose divine relationship was restored*

---

## The last Adam
In the beginning God had a perfect relationship with the first Adam. God made the first Adam and called him to

fellowship and worship Him. It was a love relationship based on faith and obedience; a relationship where the first Adam **chose** to live a life of total trust in God and total obedience to God's word. However, the second disobedience crept into the camp this perfect relationship was severed. The first Adam was not made to die but when he chose to disobey the truth of God's word he inherited the sin nature, a nature that led to both spiritual and physical death.

However, in 1 Corinthians chapter 15:45 the scriptures refer to Jesus as *The Last Adam*. Just like the first Adam, Jesus had a perfect love relationship with God, based on faith and obedience. But unlike the first Adam, the last Adam's obedience was complete. Jesus, though all God, lived on earth as all man within the boundaries of humanity, and though tempted in every way imaginable, He lived sin-free; His trust in God never wavered. When the first Adam fell divine relationship was broken but when the last Adam rose divine relationship was restored. Jesus is called the last Adam because He is the last piece of God's original plan for man. In Jesus God's plan for man is complete; there's nothing left for anyone else to do.

When Jesus walked the earth He NEVER stepped outside the limitations of humanity. Yet, in just three years He left an indelible mark on the face of the earth; He fed the hungry, healed the sick, and made the lame jump for joy. He gave sight to the blind, hearing to deaf and life to the dead. There was not a miracle under the sun that The Father did not fulfil through Jesus. Jesus simply changed every life that crossed His path. How did He do it? How was He able to accomplish all those mighty works? How could a man have such an impact on humanity?

Jesus was able to do everything He did because He

**KNEW** The Father. While on earth Jesus had an intimate relationship with The Father; a relationship so tight that Jesus talked and walked The Father's will, a relationship so deep that it made Jesus one with The Father. **Jesus had the perfect relationship with The Father because He never let go of His Father's hand.** Jesus was all God yet He humbled Himself and walked the earth as all man; *Jesus never did His own because He never walked alone!*

# RECONCILED

Afterwards taking a brief look at Abraham, Isaac, Jacob, Moses and David we clearly see how their lives paint a vivid picture of what it is like to have a personal relationship with God. But these men were special; they were chosen specifically by God Himself! *So, do we really think we stand a remote chance of having such a personal experience with The Almighty God?*

## Broken relationship

As seen in Chapters 1 & 7, the relationship that God had with the first Adam and the last Adam was on another level. In fact every other divine relationship mentioned in the Bible, be it Abraham's, Isaac's, Jacob's, Moses' or David's, was simply a shadow compared to what God shared with the Adam's. The truth is that the relationship God had with the first Adam and the last Adam was perfect. However, when the first Adam fell, that perfect relationship was broken.

> [12] *Wherefore, as by one man sin entered into the world, and death by sin; and so death passed upon all men, for that all*

*have sinned:*

*Roman 5:12*

When the first Adam disobeyed God he took on the *sin nature* and, being the progenitor of mankind, He brought death upon himself and all his posterity. In a nutshell, every human being that has graced the face of the earth sadly has this sin nature as an inheritance; Abraham, Isaac, Jacob, Moses, David, you and I, no one is exempt. As a result of the first Adam's fall God's original plan for man seemed to have taken a knock, but as usual God had it all in hand. It is important to remember that the coming of the last Adam was not an alternative plan; it was **ALWAYS** God's original plan. God is *omniscient; He knows the end from the beginning so nothing catches Him unawares.*

## First Adam, Last Adam

The first Adam is said to be a *figure* of the last Adam *{Romans 5:14}*; he was a shadow of He that was to come. This implies that, though they were similar, they were different:

> [45]*And so it is written, The first man Adam was made a living soul; the last Adam was made a quickening spirit.*

*1 Corinthians 15:45*

The scriptures describe the first Adam as a living soul. He was formed from the dust of the earth and became a living soul when God breathed into him the breath of life *{Genesis 2:7}*. Before his fall, the first Adam was innocent, sinless, and holy; he was a perfect man with a perfect walk with God. The first Adam was *posso non peccare.* Even though he was *able not to sin* he chose to sin and through him came death and condemnation.

The last Adam on the other hand, is a *"quickening"* spirit. He is a *"Spirit"* rather than a *"soul"*, and not only is He *"living"*, He is also *"life-giving"*. The last Adam is the Lord from Heaven *{1 Corinthians 15:47}*. Like the first Adam, when He walked the earth he was innocent, sinless, and holy but unlike the first Adam, He lived a life of total obedience to God. Through the last Adam man's relationship with God has been restored; through Jesus man can receive life and justification. So, though everyone died through Adam, everyone can live through Christ.

[14]*Nevertheless death reigned from Adam to Moses, even over them that had not sinned after the similitude of Adam's transgression, who is the figure of him that was to come.*

[15]*But not as the offence, so also is the free gift. For if through the offence of one many be dead, much more the grace of God, and the gift by grace, which is by one man, Jesus Christ, hath abounded unto many.*

[16]*And not as it was by one that sinned, so is the gift: for the judgment was by one to condemnation, but the free gift is of many offences unto justification.*

[17]*For if by one man's offence death reigned by one; much more they which receive abundance of grace and of the gift of righteousness shall reign in life by one, Jesus Christ.)*

[18]*Therefore as by the offence of one judgment came upon all men to condemnation; even so by the righteousness of one the free gift came upon all men unto justification of life.*

[19]*For as by one man's disobedience many were made sinners, so by the obedience of one shall many be made righteous.*

[20]*Moreover the law entered, that the offence might abound. But where sin abounded, grace did much more abound:*

[21]*That as sin hath reigned unto death, even so might grace reign through righteousness unto eternal life by Jesus Christ our Lord.*

*Romans 5:14-21*

[25]*Jesus said unto her, I am the resurrection, and the life: HE THAT BELIEVETH IN ME, THOUGH HE WERE DEAD, YET SHALL HE LIVE:*

*John 11:25*

# On the cross...

Jesus lived to die for mankind *{Romans 5:6,8}*. He knew no sin yet He died for our sins *{Galatians 1:3-4}*. He became a curse for us so as to redeem us from the curse of the law *{Galatians 3:13}*. Jesus became something He was not, so that we could become something we were not. One could say that The Prince became a pauper, so that we paupers might become princes.

> *²¹For he hath made him to be sin for us, who knew no sin; that we might be made the righteousness of God in him.*
>
> *2 Corinthians 5:21*

On the cross Jesus was pierced for our transgressions and crushed for our iniquities. He was punished so that we might have peace with God. The Father placed the sin of all men on His Son, Jesus and through His suffering and death mankind can have peace and life *{Isaiah 53:4-12}*.

On the cross Jesus won the victory over satan and his cohorts. Jesus disarmed and humiliated them and placed them on public display. Paul describes this in Colossians chapter 2:

> *¹³And you, being dead in your sins and the uncircumcision of your flesh, hath he quickened together with him, having forgiven you all trespasses;*
>
> *¹⁴Blotting out the handwriting of ordinances that was against us, which was contrary to us, and took it out of the way, nailing it to his cross;*
>
> *¹⁵AND HAVING SPOILED PRINCIPALITIES AND POWERS, HE MADE A SHEW OF THEM OPENLY, TRIUMPHING OVER THEM IN IT.*
>
> *Colossians 2:13-15*

Three days after His death, Jesus rose from the grave victorious over death; satan was rendered powerless. Jesus disarmed the one who holds the power of death

*{Hebrews 2:14}*; the key of death is no longer in satan's hands. The chain of *spiritual* death which the devil used to bind mankind is broken. Now, in Christ, we receive spiritual life; we are no longer under the dominion of the evil one. Who would have known that a shameful death on the cross would actually free mankind from the enemy's stranglehold?

---

*When we confess our sins, our slate is wiped clean before God because the precious blood of Jesus, though red, washes us white as snow*

---

Jesus paid the price for our salvation on the cross. In love, The Father gave His Son as a sacrifice for our forgiveness; in Jesus' death we find forgiveness in the sight of The Father. Years ago I once heard someone say that when we repent of sin God forgets about it; verses like Hebrews chapter 8:12 and Hebrews chapter 10:17, where God says *He will remember our sins no more*, were used to buttress this *"truth"*. I could not help but ask myself, "How does a perfect God take on the imperfection of forgetfulness; does the all knowing God really forget things?"

The truth is God can choose to do whatever He wants, whenever He wants. After all, He is God. So, He can decide to forget our sins. However, even though it may sound like a play of words, there is actually a difference between *"forgetting"* and *"remembering no more"*.

To *remember* means to bring to mind, to think of, to give attention to, or to consider. One could say to *remember* means to retrieve stored information from memory which implies that to *not remember* means not to retrieve stored information from memory. Not remembering does not mean that stored information has been lost or deleted nor does it mean that it is not retrievable. To *remember no more* simply means that though that information is retrievable it simply is not retrieved. Though the knowledge of our forgiven sins has not been deleted from God's memory, He simply sees no need to retrieve this *sinformation*.

When God says He will remember our sins no more He is saying that He will not throw them back in our face when we slip up again. The truth is God forgives, He does not forget. God forgets nothing, including our sins. When we confess our sins, they are no longer of any consequence. The price was paid when Jesus carried our sins in His body and nailed them to the cross. When we confess our sins, our slate is wiped clean before God because the precious blood of Jesus, though red, washes us white as snow.

> [7]*Blessed and happy and to be envied are those whose iniquities are forgiven and whose sins are covered up and completely buried.*
> [8]*Blessed and happy and to be envied is the person of whose sin the Lord will take no account nor reckon it against him.*
>
> Romans 4:7-8 {AMP}

On the cross Jesus reconciled man to God the Father. This, I believe is the primary reason why the Word became flesh, the reason why God became man and lived with us; the reason why the One who knew no sin took on our sins so that every sinner could once again walk hand in hand with The Father.

---

*God has always loved man. The Cross was a pure show of real love; the completion of God's reconciliation plan.*

---

A relationship with man has always ranked high on God's priority list but the sin factor was always a hindrance. As you may have heard over and over again, the truth is that God loves the sinner but simply cannot stand the sin. God's love for mankind has never dwindled and as seen in Romans chapter 5 and John chapter 3, God did not wait for man to make a move towards Him {*He most likely would have waited forever!*}. In love, God paved a way for man to come back to Him by giving the life of His only begotten Son.

> [6]*For when we were yet without strength, in due time Christ died for the ungodly.*
> [7]*For scarcely for a righteous man will one die: yet peradventure for a good man some would even dare to die.*
> [8]*But God commendeth his love toward us, in that, while we were yet sinners, Christ died for us.*
>
> *Romans 5:6-8*

> [16]*For God so loved the world, that he gave his only begotten Son, that whosoever believeth in him should not perish, but have everlasting life.*
> [17]*For God sent not his Son into the world to condemn the world; but that the world through him might be saved.*
>
> *John 3:16-17*

Man has never had to force God's hand to see His love. God has always loved man. The Cross was a pure show of real love; the completion of God's reconciliation plan. Jesus died to save all mankind and free man from the enemy's hold. If man chooses to live in Christ the perfect divine relationship, broken by Adam, would once again be restored.

## In Christ
Salvation was made available by Christ, and it is only available to man through faith in Him {*Acts 4:10-12*}. When Jesus paid the ransom ~ *the equivalent, corresponding*

*price* ~ for mankind, He became man's only way into the presence of The Father *{John 14:5-7}.* Jesus did not come to negotiate; He did not come to bargain or to compromise God's standards on our behalf. Jesus came to mediate; He came to reconcile and bridge the gap between God and man. Jesus opened the door to God's mercy without compromising God's righteous standards. God the Son took humanity upon Himself that He might take humanity back to God the Father. You and I can once again have a personal relationship with God if we live our lives in Christ.

---

*When we live in Christ we have everything; when we live in Christ we are complete*

---

From scripture we see Jesus Christ as the Only Begotten Son of God, the Son of man, the Author of life, the Author and Perfecter of our faith, Alpha and Omega, the Beginning and the End, the First and the Last, the Heir of all things, the Creator of all things, the all-sufficient Saviour, the all-sufficient Mediator, the Chief Cornerstone, the Chief Shepherd, the Great High Priest, the Wisdom of God, the Word of God, the Way, the Truth, the Resurrection, the Life, the King of kings, the Lord of lords,.... the list goes on and on. However, to cap it all off, in the book of Colossians Jesus is called **THE FULLNESS OF THE GODHEAD** *{Colossians 2:10}*; **HE IS ALL, AND IN ALL** *{Colossians 3:11}.* Nothing can be added and nothing can go beyond Christ. Simply put, **JESUS CHRIST IS COMPLETE!** When we live in Christ we have everything; when we live in Christ we are complete.

> [8] *Beware lest any man spoil you through philosophy and vain deceit, after the tradition of men, after the rudiments of the world, and not after Christ.*

*⁹FOR IN HIM DWELLETH ALL THE FULNESS OF THE GODHEAD bodily.*

*¹⁰And YE ARE COMPLETE IN HIM, which is the head of all principality and power:*

Colossians 2:8-10

So many times we find ourselves saying that if one does not give their life to Christ and get born again then they make the death of Christ of no effect. This is true but taking a closer look I dare say that anyone who has given their life to Christ but does not live their life in Christ is most likely wearing the same shoes. Now, before jumping to the conclusion that this paragraph has nothing to do with you let us take a brief look at who we are in Christ. In Christ...

...we are justified

*{Romans 5:1}*

...we are given a right standing with God

*{2 Corinthians 5:21}*

...we are new creations

*{2 Corinthians 5:17}*

...we have access to the grace of God

*{Romans 5:2}*

...we are children of God

*{John 1:12}*

...we are no longer condemned

*{Romans 8:1}*

...we are free from the law of sin and death

*{Roman 8:2}*

...we are reconciled to God

*{2 Corinthians 5:18-19}*

...we are redeemed

*{Colossians 1:13-14}*

...we are forgiven

*{Colossians 1:13-14}*

...we are saved by grace through faith
*{Ephesians 2:8}*
...we are friends of God
*{John15:13}*
...we can call God Abba Father
*{Romans 8:15}*
...we are chosen by God
*{1 Peter 2:9}*
...we are a royal priesthood
*{1 Peter 2:9}*
...we are one with The Father
*{Acts17:28}*

...we are healed
*{1 Peter 2:24}*
...we can do all things
*{Philippians 4:13}*
...we are overcomers
*{Revelation 12:11}*
...we are more than conquerors
*{Romans 8:37}*
...we lack no need
*{Philippians 4:19}*
...we have power and authority over the enemy
*{Luke 10:17}*
...we are blessed with every spiritual blessing
*{Ephesians 1:3}*
...we display God's wonderful deeds
*{1 Peter 2:9}*
...we have eternal life
*{1 John 5:11-12}*
...we are safe and secure in God
*{Colossians 3:3}*
...we are never alone
*{Hebrews 13:5}*

...we have access to the Spirit of God
{*Romans 8:11*}
In Christ we are complete!
{*Colossians 2:10*}


Now, let us be real. Ask yourself, "*Do I really understand what it means to live in Christ?*" If you do then ask yourself, "*How much of my life am I actually living in Christ?*" Being honest, when I got to this part of the book I had to drop my pen. I took a good look at who I am *supposed to be* in Christ and I could not help but ask myself, "*What right do I have writing these words when I myself am still struggling to live my life in Christ*". But a little later I heard the voice of God say, "**Remember, knowing the truth will set you free. At the moment you may not be walking in the totality of The Truth but, the more truth you know and understand the more of it you will walk in**". So, once again I picked up my pen.

IN CHRIST WE ARE FORGIVEN; we no longer stand before God as debtors because in Jesus the debt has been paid {Ephesians 1:7}. IN CHRIST WE ARE REDEEMED; we no longer stand before God as slaves because in Jesus freedom has been granted {*Romans 8:19-22*}. IN CHRIST WE ARE JUSTIFIED; we no longer stand before God condemned and guilty because in Jesus we are declared righteous {*Romans 8:33*}. IN CHRIST WE ARE ADOPTED; we no longer stand before God as strangers because in Jesus we have become His sons {*Ephesians 1:5*}. IN CHRIST WE ARE RECONCILED; we are no longer enemies with God because in Jesus we are His friends {*2 Corinthians 5:18-20*}.

# TOUCHING
# THE FATHER'S HEART
## *A Closer Relationship*

For God so loved the world that He gave His only begotten Son, that whosoever believes in Him should not perish, but have everlasting life". God loved man so much that He gave His one and only Son to reconcile man back to Himself. The love God has for us is so great that He gave Jesus, *the fullness of the Godhead,* so that the relationship He once shared with man could be restored. In fact the love God displayed to bring man back to Him is described as the greatest love of all:

> *[13]GREATER LOVE HATH NO MAN THAN THIS, THAT A MAN LAY DOWN HIS LIFE FOR HIS FRIENDS.*

> *John 15:13*

God put Himself through the pain of giving up His only Son simply because He wants to have a relationship with us; this may not be easy to comprehend but it is the truth. To make it a bit more *unbelievable,* what would run through your mind if I told you that God does not just want a Father-son or Master-servant relationship with us. He also desires something a lot closer, something a lot more fruitful; God wants us to be **HIS TRUE FRIENDS.**

Alright, but are we not pushing things a bit too far here? After all, we are talking about the same God; the One who is perfection personified, who created everything yet was not created, who lives in utter splendour, whom the oceans applaud and all creation declare His grandeur, the One who is an awesome wonder. Yes, but remember that He is also the same God who broke down every conceivable barrier that stands between us and Him, who lovingly gave His Son that we may be reconciled to Him, who forgave our sins and openly invited us to come to Him; the same God who paid the priceless price that we may once again enter into His presence.

---

*Jesus called His disciples friends because He could confide in them everything His Father told Him*

---

## True friendship

Webster's Unabridged Dictionary defines a friend as "*a person who gives assistance; a person who is on good terms with another; a person whom one knows, likes, and trusts*". It therefore would not be out of place to say that true friends like to be with each other, can be themselves with each other, confide in each other, forgive each other, are always there for each other, and go the extra mile for each other. However, the characteristic of true friendship that ties all these together is the fact that TRUE FRIENDS KNOW EACH OTHER. It is almost impossible to call someone your friend if you hardly know anything about the person. This is emphasised in John chapter 15 where Jesus is talking to His disciples.

Jesus had started rounding up His earthly ministry. It was just before the feast of The Passover; Jesus had washed His disciple's dirty feet and was now sharing from His heart before His crucifixion. Jesus had walked with His disciples from the beginning of His ministry so I believe it is safe to say that by now He knew each one of them inside out. Also, the disciples had spent quality time in Jesus' presence {Mark 3:14} and knew that their Master was no ordinary man. The disciples believed in Jesus and knew that truly He was the Son of God. Up till now the relationship that existed between Jesus and His disciples had been a Master-servant relationship. However, as Jesus' last days on earth drew near, this was all about to change:

> [15]*Henceforth I call you not servants; for the servant knoweth not what his lord doeth: but I have called you friends; for all things that I have heard of my Father I have made known unto you.*

> *John 15:15*

Here Jesus was not abolishing the Master-servant relationship which He spoke of in John chapter 13:13-16. Jesus simply believed it was time to let His disciples know that, after walking and working together, and getting to know each other over the past three years they had become a lot more than servants. In a sense Jesus was telling His disciples that He was taking their relationship to the next level; THE LEVEL OF FRIENDSHIP. Jesus goes on to explain the reason for this relationship status change: "*for all things that I have heard of my Father I have made known unto you.*"

From His words, His works and simply being in His presence the disciples had come to know Jesus. Likewise, Jesus knew His disciples and trusted them enough to pour Himself into them. JESUS CALLED HIS DISCIPLES FRIENDS BECAUSE HE COULD CONFIDE IN THEM EVERYTHING HIS FATHER TOLD HIM; something He would not have done if He only saw them as servants. It goes without saying that to be called a friend of God we need to know God. The big question however is, "**HOW?**"

## Spiritual intimacy

It has been said that it was a lot easier for those in the Old Testament to do what God told them because they actually heard His voice audibly, and it was even easier, at least for those who believed, to walk with God when Jesus was around because they could actually see God in *the flesh*. However, nowadays His voice is not exactly "*audible*" and seeing Him in the flesh is a bit farfetched. So, as believers, how do we get to know God?

### - The Spirit of Truth

Hundreds of books have been written, and thousands of messages preached about Him so I guess when it comes to the Holy Spirit most of us have heard it all. But let me briefly share with you my two pence.

As Jesus' earthly ministry came to an end He promised His disciples that He would not leave them alone. Jesus said He would ask The Father to give another Comforter, One that will be with them forever. This Comforter was the Spirit of truth *{John 14:16-20}*.

WHEN JESUS THE COMFORTER ASCENDED TO BE WITH THE FATHER, HOLY SPIRIT THE COMFORTER DESCENDED TO BE WITH EVERY BELIEVER. Jesus said that, "*...the Comforter, which is the Holy Ghost, whom the Father will send in my name, He shall teach you all things, and bring all things to your remembrance, whatsoever I have said unto you*". As long as we walk hand in hand with the Holy Ghost we will take on the mind of Christ.

Apart from being our Comforter we see from scripture that the Holy Ghost is also our Guide *{John 16:13}*, our

Counsellor and our Teacher *{John 14:26}*. As Sons of God He is there to lead us *{Romans 8:14}* and He even helps us out when we intercede *{Romans 8:26}*. Jesus clearly states in the book of Acts chapter 1:8 that *we receive power when the Holy Ghost comes upon us*, thus making us understand that with the Holy Ghost we can do *"the impossible"*.

---

## *When we give ourselves to God's Spirit the door to God's mind is open to us*

---

In 1 Corinthians chapter 2 we also see that the Holy Spirit is ALL-KNOWING and through Him we have the ability to actually know the things of God:

> *⁹But as it is written, Eye hath not seen, nor ear heard, neither have entered into the heart of man, the things which God hath prepared for them that love him.*
> *¹⁰BUT GOD HATH REVEALED THEM UNTO US BY HIS SPIRIT: FOR THE SPIRIT SEARCHETH ALL THINGS, YEA, THE DEEP THINGS OF GOD.*
> *¹¹FOR WHAT MAN KNOWETH THE THINGS OF A MAN, SAVE THE SPIRIT OF MAN WHICH IS IN HIM? EVEN SO THE THINGS OF GOD KNOWETH NO MAN, BUT THE SPIRIT OF GOD.*
> *¹²NOW WE HAVE RECEIVED, NOT THE SPIRIT OF THE WORLD, BUT THE SPIRIT WHICH IS OF GOD; THAT WE MIGHT KNOW THE THINGS THAT ARE FREELY GIVEN TO US OF GOD.*
> *¹⁶For who hath known the mind of the Lord, that he may instruct him? but we have the mind of Christ.*
>
> *1 Corinthians 2:9-12; 16*

What makes all this so exciting is the truth that the Holy Spirit lives in us; WE ARE TEMPLES OF GOD AND THE SPIRIT OF GOD DWELLS IN US *{1 Corinthians 3:16}*. This simply means that if we choose to flow with the Spirit of God within us we are able to know the will of God concerning every situation. When we give ourselves to God's Spirit the door to God's mind is open to us. Hence we find ourselves thinking God's thoughts because we have the mind of Christ.

Only the Spirit of God knows the deep things of God and only the Spirit of God can reveal these deep things of God. As believers The Holy Spirit is in us; we carry Him around sixty seconds every minute, sixty minutes every hour, twenty four hours every day, seven days every week, fifty two weeks every year. He is always with us! However, though He is always there can we say that He plays an active part in our day to day lives, or is He simply the dormant third person of The Trinity?

The truth is that for too long many of us have seen the Holy Spirit as a tool that God gave us to use in time of need hence the reason why we see the Holy Spirit as an "it" rather than a "He". If we understood that He is actually a member of the Godhead, *one with God the Father and God the Son*, then maybe we would see Him in a different light.

With the Holy Spirit in us we have the ability to do, not just the works that Jesus did when He walked the earth but, greater works. It is time for us to wake up to the reality of the presence of the Holy Spirit in us. When we do we will begin to walk in the deep things of God and, with a willing and obedient heart, we will touch The Father's heart.

### *- To know Him, to love Him:*
From 2 Timothy we come to understand that every word of scripture is inspired by God Himself {*2 Timothy 3:16*}. This implies that the scriptures, the written word, or maybe I should just say "*The Bible*" is simply the inspired word of

God. I personally believe that it is simply amazing that God would reveal Himself to fallible writers by the Holy Spirit, for truly *what is man that God is so mindful of him?* It just goes to show how precious we are in God's sight. Even though God is sovereign and can easily accomplish all things without the assistance of any other, He still chooses to give man such a big part to play in His plan.

It is also exciting to know that God and His word are one. So, each time we look into the Bible we are actually looking at God's mind, His character, and His works penned on paper. Whenever we look into the scriptures with the help of the Holy Spirit the Word of God comes to life. When we look into God's word with the help of the Holy Spirit we come to know more about God Himself. Take a look at what God told Joshua:

> *⁸This book of the law shall not depart out of thy mouth; but thou shalt meditate therein day and night, that thou mayest observe to do according to all that is written therein: for then thou shalt make thy way prosperous, and then thou shalt have good success.*
>
> *Joshua 1:8*

God commands Joshua to keep meditating on His word both day and night. He makes Joshua realise that the more he meditates the more he will know what to do. God then gave Joshua the guarantee that as long as he does all that is written in The Word he would witness prosperity and good success. The truth is the more we chew on God's word, the more we see God. The more we see God, the more we know Him. The more we know God, the more we want to live to please Him. The more we live to please God, the more He brings prosperity and good success our way.

God's plan was never to hide from man. If it was He

would never have given us the Holy Spirit and His Word in the first place. Going back to the Garden of Eden we see that man is the one who does all the hiding. God created us to have a loving relationship with Him and, even though we fell, God pulled out all the stops to ensure that once again we be reconciled to Him. The closer we look the more we see that God desires that we grow to know Him. In John chapter 17 Jesus makes us realise that the reason why He did what He did was so that we would come to know God.

> [3]*And this is life eternal, THAT THEY MIGHT KNOW THEE THE ONLY TRUE GOD, AND JESUS CHRIST, WHOM THOU HAST SENT.*
>
> *John 17:3*

The importance God places on knowing Him is further highlighted in Jeremiah chapter 9:

> [23]*Thus saith the LORD, Let not the wise man glory in his wisdom, neither let the mighty man glory in his might, let not the rich man glory in his riches:*
> [24]*But let him that glorieth glory in this, THAT HE UNDERSTANDETH AND KNOWETH ME, that I am the LORD which exercise lovingkindness, judgment, and righteousness, in the earth: for in these things I delight, saith the LORD.*
>
> *Jeremiah 9:23-24*

Here God makes it clear that only one person has a right to brag; the one who understands and knows Him, the one who has a personal relationship with Him and recognises His character, the one who constantly delves into His Word receiving illumination from the Holy Spirit.

---

*... the person who desires, seeks, cherishes and keeps God's Word comes to know God's character and will; that person comes to know God*

---

Psalm 119 is one psalm written from the heart of one who cherished the Word of God. Even though the name of the psalmist is concealed I believe this psalm was written by David, someone who desired to continually seek God {Psalm 119:12, 18,135}; one with a heart after God. From this Psalm it is obvious that the psalmist understood that God's Word represented His Name, His character and His will. We also see that the psalmist was passionate about obeying God's Word; obeying God's commandments, judgements, laws, precepts and statutes.

From this Psalm we see that the person who desires, seeks, cherishes and keeps God's Word is considered blessed, happy, fortunate, and is to be envied {Psalm 119:1-2}; has great understanding {Psalm 119:98-100, 104}; learns how to live right {Psalm 119:9-11}; receives salvation {Psalm 119:155}, direction and illumination {Psalm 119:105}. But more importantly, the person who desires, seeks, cherishes and keeps God's Word comes to know God's character and will; that person comes to know God.

God wants to have a personal, face to face relationship with each of us, hence the reason why He wants us to know Him and not just know about Him. God desires that we know Him because He wants us to love Him with all that is within us {Mark 12:29-33}, thus making *His first commandment* a loving, heartfelt decision rather than a chore.

---

*God's word also reveals God's plan for man and how man can live a life that is truly pleasing and acceptable in God's sight*

---

When God commands us to love Him with all our heart,

soul, mind and strength it is important for us to see that He is not saying that these are four different ways of loving Him. Here is the catch; *we cannot love God with all our heart if we do not love Him with all our soul, we cannot love God with all our soul if we do not love Him with all our mind, and we cannot love God with all our mind if we do not love Him with all our strength;* they are all intertwined. The more we fill our minds with God's word, with the help of the Holy Spirit, the more we come to know Him. The more we come to know Him, the more we grow to love Him. But it does not end there because the more we grow to love Him, the more we want to seek Him through His word. It is an unending cycle that yields eternal rewards.

God's love for us is mind blowing; He calls us the apple of His eye *{Zechariah 2:8}*, He says that we are always on His mind *{Isaiah 49:15}*; He even says that our names are engraved on the palm of His hand *{Isaiah 49:16}*. God loves us so much that He gave His only begotten Son for us. The more we grow to know God the more we realise how great His love for us is. The more we understand how much He loves us the more, and easier it becomes, to love Him. The truth is that God loved us first with an everlasting love so that we could come to know Him, and love Him.

God's Word reveals Who God is. God's Word reveals how to know God. God's word also reveals God's plan for man and how man can live a life that is truly pleasing and acceptable in God's sight. We come to know more of God as the Holy Spirit reveals the character and mind of God to us through God's written word. The more we read and meditate on God's Word with a heart that truly wants to know more about God, the greater the tendency of God's Word being revealed to us by the Holy Spirit.

This, in turn, causes our love for God to grow deeper. The more we know God, the more we love God, the more we touch God's heart.

*- Born to worship:*
The two primary words that are used to describe *"worship"* in the Bible are the Hebrew word **"shahhah"**, used mainly in the Old Testament, and the Greek word **"Proskuneo"**, used more than 50 times in the New Testament. Interestingly both words share a similar meaning: *to bow down, crouch, kneel, fall down, humbly beseech, do obeisance, do reverence, to put one's face down as an act of respect and submission, prostrate in homage to royalty or God.*

In the Old Testament worship almost always took place at certain times, in certain places, in certain ways. In fact, sometimes you get the feeling that the people might have found themselves focussing more on the *"rituals of worship"* instead of God, the *"object of worship"*. However, in the New Testament Jesus shakes things up a bit. In John chapter 4 we see Jesus remove the limitations that had been placed on worship:

> [20] *Our fathers worshipped in this mountain; and ye say, that in Jerusalem is the place where men ought to worship.*
> [21] *Jesus saith unto her, Woman, believe me, the hour cometh, when ye shall neither in this mountain, nor yet at Jerusalem, worship the Father.*
> [22] *Ye worship ye know not what: we know what we worship: for salvation is of the Jews.*
> [23] *But the hour cometh, and now is, when the TRUE WORSHIPPERS SHALL WORSHIP THE FATHER IN SPIRIT AND IN TRUTH: FOR THE FATHER SEEKETH SUCH TO WORSHIP HIM.*
> [24] *GOD IS A SPIRIT: AND THEY THAT WORSHIP HIM MUST WORSHIP HIM IN SPIRIT AND IN TRUTH.*

> *John 4:20-24*

Inasmuch as Jesus talks about having the right attitude *{a real, genuine and sincere attitude}* before God, He also emphasises the truth that God is a Spirit. God is not limited by time and space. God is everywhere, every time and if we truly believe in His omnipresence then it should dawn on us that there are no limitations on when and where we can worship God. We can worship our Father anywhere, and at anytime. We also come to realise that even though worship always seems to have an outward response, true worship always stems from the heart.

---

## *True worship ceases to exist where there is no relationship*

---

Reading through John chapter 4 we see Jesus get into a discussion with a Samaritan woman at Jacob's well. He presents Himself as the Living Water; as Everlasting Life! *{vs.13-14}*. He then goes on to make her realise that it is not possible to truly worship when she has no knowledge or understanding of whom or what she worships *{vs.22}*. It is only after this that Jesus brings up the issue of *"true worship by true worshippers"*.

In the context of John chapter 4 we see that true worship can only be offered by true worshippers; by those who know *whom* they worship. A true worshipper is someone who has drunk the living water and has received eternal life. A true worshipper is someone who believes in Jesus Christ and has submitted his heart to Him. A true worshipper is someone who trusts and believes in Jesus, the Way, the Truth, and the Life. A true worshipper is someone who knows that the only true way to the heart of the one true God is through Jesus. A true worshipper is someone who has a heart relationship with the Father.

Something that can so easily be missed in these verses is the truth that God is not primarily looking for *"true worship"* {vs.23}; He is actually looking for *"true worshippers"*; He is not looking for the *"act of worship"*, He is looking for a *"heart of worship"*. Believe it or not, but what God desires the most is a relationship with you. Just like Jesus pointed out to the woman by the well, you cannot offer true worship to someone you do not know. The reason why God is looking for true worshippers is simply because a true worshipper has a heart for God. True worship ceases to exist where there is no relationship.

Man was created to fellowship with God; he was created to worship God. Every part of man, his spirit, his soul, his mind, his body is wired to glorify God. This simply means that though primarily we worship from our spirit, true worship also involves having the right mind attitude, which should naturally create the right body actions.

> [4] *And round about the throne were four and twenty seats: and upon the seats I saw four and twenty elders sitting, clothed in white raiment; and they had on their heads crowns of gold.*
> [10] *The four and twenty elders fall down before him that sat on the throne, and worship him that liveth for ever and ever, and cast their crowns before the throne, saying,*
> [11] *Thou art worthy, O Lord, to receive glory and honour and power: for thou hast created all things, and for thy pleasure they are and were created.*
>
> **Revelation 4:4,10-11**

All through the book of Revelation we see *"worship"* scenes where the twenty four elders who sat before the throne continually worshipped The Lamb {5:8-14, 7:11-12, 11:16-17, 19:4} and not once did their worship include anything personal. They submitted to Him, praised and adored Him, declared His worthiness and celebrated His presence. The sole focus of their worship was God.

We do not worship God in order to obtain our needs or His blessings. We do not worship God so as to feel spiritual or even to *feel* His presence. We worship God simply because of who He is: GOD! Even if God chose not to meet our needs or if He did not bless us, the mind of a true worshipper should remain focussed on God.

> [1]*I beseech you therefore, brethren, by the mercies of God, that ye present your bodies a living sacrifice, holy, acceptable unto God, which is your reasonable service.*
>
> *Romans 12:1*

Just as He presented Himself as a sacrifice for us, we too must present our bodies as a living sacrifice for Him. EVERYTHING we do, the seeds we sow, the service we offer, the show of concern for others, the very lives we live, should actually be done with the purpose of bringing glory to God. Could one therefore say that "worship is a lifestyle"? Here is an illustration that was dropped in my heart a while back.

---

*We must not make the mistake of limiting our worship to the songs of praise we sing and what we do at a Sunday service*

---

The one thing we know we will definitely do when we get to heaven is worship our Father. Does this mean that all we will ever do is sing? Maybe, but somehow I do not think so. For a split second let us assume that the earth we live in right now is Heaven *{I know this is not the easiest of tasks but let us try and put our imagination to work}*. If we say that worship is a lifestyle, that is the way we live our lives, then it would imply that the things we do every day, be it sleeping, praying, working or playing, etc would somehow make up our worship to God. Do you get my drift?

Though we are far from perfect we should not take it lightly that God is first and foremost interested in our hearts. Once your heart is right you can begin the journey. Even in our imperfect state, the desire and cry of every believer, every true worshipper, should be, *"Father, everything I do I do to please You"*. At times this is all a bit too much to comprehend so in order to simplify things we tend to take the easy way out: keep God in church, and out of our everyday lives. So, we live a life of worship on a Sunday but come Monday, God's place in our daily activities is limited to the barest minimum.

We need to come to a place where we understand God's omnipresence, and start to remove the limitations that we have placed on our worship of the One True God. We must not make the mistake of limiting our worship to the songs of praise we sing and what we do at a Sunday service. We must ensure that our worship breaks through the church's four walls and truly becomes the life we live.

The heart of a true worshipper remains faithful to God, the mind of a true worshipper remains focussed on God, and the body of a true worshipper continually lives for God. True worship can only come from the heart of a true worshipper. True worship from the heart of a true worshipper ALWAYS touches the Father's heart.

### - *Spend some time with Me:*
There are various kinds of prayer, most of which I believe a lot of us may already be familiar with. The prayer of petition and supplication *{where we make honest, heartfelt requests to God}*, the prayer of intercession {where one comes before God to plead on behalf of another}, the prayer of praise and adoration *{when we honour God*

*through the exaltation of who He is}*, and the prayer of thanksgiving *{where we simply acknowledge the things that God has done; something that we so often tend to take for granted!}*, are a few that readily come to mind. However, rather than dwell on the different types of prayer I would like us to ask ourselves this question: "How can I effectively communicate the content of my heart to God?"

When it comes to the subject of prayer I know there is no shortage of material. If asked to define prayer, definitions abound. However the meaning of prayer that has stuck with me for quite awhile is this: PRAYER IS HAVING DIALOGUE WITH GOD. More and more I seem to realise that prayer is not just a time to talk to God; it is a time to talk with Him. Also, something else that increasingly comes to light is that prayer is not just about talking; it has a lot to do with listening too.

I remember when I was growing up. I would go to church and, even though I had not asked Jesus into my heart, I sometimes got the feeling that the *acts of worship* carried out were just too stereotyped. Meaning no disrespect, but I remember the prayers I used to recite from the church prayer book; now, I cannot speak on behalf of anyone else but I do not really think I meant a word of what I said. I definitely did not think I was connecting with my Heavenly Father. It was simply an every Sunday chore which I had to carry out as a *"Christian"*.

Now, we could argue and say, "I was not born again so I really did not have a clue", which is true but guess what happened when I finally got saved. Sure, there was a lot more variety and there was definitely a lot more activity, which was fun. But the further I walked down my Christian pathway the more my religious thinking seemed to lock God in a box. Somehow I got it into my head that there were *certain* ways to pray, *certain* times to pray and *certain* things to pray about *{does that sound familiar?}*. At times I even found myself having thoughts like, *"if only I knew this was going to happen I would have included it in my morning quiet time. Well, I guess I'll just have to pray about it during my next quiet session.* For some reason I had this silly mindset that was ignorant to the fact that the One I was praying to was the all knowing, in all places at all times God.

---

*...inasmuch as God wants to hear from us He also wants us to hear from Him*

---

When it came to prayer one of my downfalls was that I thought I had to do all the talking, and since I did not expect God to say anything anyway, listening really was not part of the equation. However, the day I came to understand that sound relationships are built on the foundation of sound communication things changed. If God has gone through so much to ensure that we have a personal relationship with Him then somehow effective communication must rank rather high on His priority list. This implies that communicating effectively with God is something we dare not take for granted.

Here lies the catch. Just like He told Abram in Genesis chapter 17:1, God wants you to empty yourself before Him, not in fear but totally secure in His love. God wants you to tell Him everything about yourself as if He knows nothing about you. Your Father never gets tired of hearing your voice, even if it is a croak. He wants you to share everything with Him; your joys, your hurts, your successes, your concerns. Even though our Father knows He still wants to know. Maybe that explains why He does not mind us praying without ceasing.

I no longer believe that the only time it is necessary to talk to God is in a time of trouble, or in time of need. Personally I believe God wants to hear my voice a lot more. He is interested in listening to us in time of joy and success too. Talking to God when the last door has just been slammed shut in your face might not be our Father's idea of perfect timing. God wants to be our first resort rather than our last resort. He calls us the apple of His eye; He always has our best interest at heart.

> [11]*For I know the thoughts that I think toward you, saith the LORD, thoughts of peace, and not of evil, to give you an expected end.*
> [12]*Then shall ye call upon me, and ye shall go and pray unto me, and I will hearken unto you.*
> [13]*And ye shall seek me, and find me, when ye shall search for me with all your heart.*
>
> *Jeremiah 29:11-13*

Nothing is too little or too much to talk to God about; NOTHING! Our Father makes it clear in His word that He is interested in our every care {1 Peter 5:7} and, even though a situation may seem impossible, He is in the business of solving impossibilities {Matthew 19:24-26}. Sometimes we hesitate to talk to God out of fear; fear that He might clamp down on our requests. To be honest there is the possibility that this could be the case because like God Himself tells us in the book of Isaiah, *"My thoughts are not your thoughts, neither are your ways My ways"{Isaiah 55:8-9}.* But, as I mentioned earlier, our all-knowing Father always has our best interest at heart. He knows us inside out, even more than we know ourselves. So, would it not be a bit daft if we chose not to talk to God about a situation, a concern or a need when He is actually the only one who holds the key?

Take a look at Matthew chapter 7:

> *⁹Or what man is there of you, whom if his son ask bread, will he give him a stone?*
> *¹⁰Or if he ask a fish, will he give him a serpent?*
> *¹¹If ye then, being evil, know how to give good gifts unto your children, how much more shall your Father which is in heaven give good things to them that ask him?*
>
> *Matthew 7:9-11*

When we approach our Father about a need or a concern He may not give us what we want or tell us what we want to hear but whatever He gives or says is perfect; something we always come to realise at the end of the day.

Another thing to remember is that inasmuch as God wants to hear from us He also wants us to hear from Him. We need to consciously expect to hear from God. Remember, prayer is dialogue; a conversation between God and you. When we talk to God about a trouble or a concern, more often than not, we require guidance or a solution to a situation. This only comes when we hear a word from God. But if we do not expect to hear from God then how do we intend to take the next step? God holds the solution to every situation. Take a look at what happens when David speaks to God:

> *²Therefore DAVID ENQUIRED OF THE LORD, saying, Shall I go and smite these Philistines? AND THE LORD SAID unto David, Go, and smite the Philistines, and save Keilah.*
> *³And David's men said unto him, Behold, we be afraid here in Judah: how much more then if we come to Keilah against the armies of the Philistines?*
> *⁴Then DAVID ENQUIRED OF THE LORD yet again. AND THE LORD ANSWERED HIM AND SAID, Arise, go down to Keilah; for I will deliver the Philistines into thine hand.*
> *⁵So David and his men went to Keilah, and fought with the Philistines, and brought away their cattle, and smote them*

*with a great slaughter. So David saved the inhabitants of Keilah.*

*1 Samuel 23:2-5*

[10]*Then said David, O LORD God of Israel, thy servant hath certainly heard that Saul seeketh to come to Keilah, to destroy the city for my sake.*
[11]*Will the men of Keilah deliver me up into his hand? will Saul come down, as thy servant hath heard? O LORD God of Israel, I beseech thee, tell thy servant. And the LORD said, He will come down.*
[12]*THEN SAID DAVID, Will the men of Keilah deliver me and my men into the hand of Saul? AND THE LORD SAID, They will deliver thee up.*

*1 Samuel 23:10-12*

---

## What David heard in the place of prayer was always the key to a breakthrough

---

Each time David *enquired of the Lord* God responded. What David heard in the place of prayer was always the key to a breakthrough. We see similar situations in the lives of Abraham *{Genesis 18:22-33}* and Moses *{Exodus 33:12-23}*. Be it through His word, His voice or a nudge from His Spirit, we should approach God with an ear to hear. We should always leave the place of prayer with an expectation of a manifestation.

From the first verse of Luke chapter 11 we once again see the importance of talking to God with an expectation to hear from Him.

[1]*And it came to pass, that, as he was praying in a certain place, when he ceased, ONE OF HIS DISCIPLES SAID UNTO HIM, LORD, TEACH US TO PRAY, AS JOHN ALSO TAUGHT HIS DISCIPLES.*
[2]*AND HE SAID UNTO THEM, WHEN YE PRAY, SAY, Our Father which art in heaven, Hallowed be thy name. Thy*

*kingdom come. Thy will be done, as in heaven, so in earth.*

Here Jesus was teaching His disciples how to pray but, even though they were His disciples, Jesus was not the one who offered to teach them. It was a disciple who spoke the desire of his heart, he expectantly made his request known, *"Lord, teach us to pray..."*, and the next thing we know the disciples expectation was being met. Now I know Jesus knew His disciples would one day ask Him to teach them how to pray but assuming they did not ask, could that mean that what we know as *"The Lord's Prayer"* would not have been recorded in scripture?

A Christian friend of mine once asked me, "Since God is all-knowing and He already knows what we need, do we really have to pray and tell Him things He already knows?" I responded to her question with a question of my own, "Is it possible to build a heartfelt relationship with someone you do not talk to?" Our Father has called us to a place of relationship; a place where we can ask Him about what He wants, a place where we can seek His guidance, a place where we can actually commune with Him. It is also a place where we can talk with Him about our wants and needs, but it is amazing how these seem to fade into the background when you are enjoying the Father's presence.

---

**Prayer is an expression of our worship to God.**

---

I was listening to a song the other day called *"Spend some time with Me"*; a song written by Ben Tankard and featuring the Tribe of Benjamin. As I listened to it over and over again my eyes seemed to swell up. The song simply painted a vivid picture of God's ever present

Touching the Father's Heart | 127

presence, how much He cares and loves us, and how much He misses us when we chose not to spend some time with Him. It went a little something like this:

I will be with you till the end
You can count on Me to be your friend
Won't you spend some time with Me
I will hold you tight in My arms
Keeping you safe from all harm
I love you spend some time with Me
{I miss you}

I will walk with you in the sand
Talking with you as we hold hands
When you spend some time with me
I will give My all from the start
All I ask of you is your heart
Won't you spend some time with Me
{I miss you}

You see Me make the sun shine so bright
I even hung the moon out at night
For you so spend some time with Me
You felt the wind I blew through the trees
You saw the ways I made in the sea
For you so spend some time with Me
{I miss you}

©Ben Tankard

Prayer is an expression of our worship to God. Knowing that God is omnipresent should make us realise that we can talk with God anytime and anywhere. The truth is that there is no restriction on how, when or where to talk with our Father, and because our Father is all-knowing and all-powerful we have the added assurance that when we talk with Him we simply cannot go wrong. The relationship that we share with our Father will grow to mind blowing heights as long as we continually come to

Him in faith and talk with Him earnestly from our hearts *{Hebrews 11:6, James 5:16b}.*

# ...And Just Before I Go

If there is one thing I would want you to grasp from the pages of this book it is this: **There is nothing more important than your relationship with God.** God made us to worship and fellowship with Him. He loves us so much that He sent His only begotten Son to bring us back to Him. God cherishes the relationship He shares with us so much that He lovingly pours Himself into us so that we can willingly live our lives for Him.

---

*... no job, no riches, no relationship, and no Godly service can take the place of a one to one, face to face relationship with God*

---

We should never make the mistake of getting our work for God mixed up with our walk with God. Nowadays it is so easy to get caught up in *"God's work"* that we actually forget all about living our lives for God. The truth is work for God that is not birthed out of a relationship with God might just be work in vain. We cannot work our way into God's heart. God himself makes this clear in Revelation chapter 2:

> *²I know your industry and activities, laborious toil and trouble, and your patient endurance, and how you cannot tolerate wicked [men] and have tested and critically appraised those who call [themselves] apostles (special messengers of Christ) and yet are not, and have found them to be impostors and liars.*
>
> *³I know you are enduring patiently and are bearing up for My name's sake, and you have not fainted or become exhausted or grown weary.*
>
> *⁴But I have this [one charge to make] against you: that you have left (abandoned) the love that you had at first [you have deserted Me, your first love].*
>
> *⁵Remember then from what heights you have fallen. Repent (change the inner man to meet God's will) and do the works you did previously [when first you knew the Lord], or else I will visit you and remove your lampstand from its place, unless you change your mind and repent.*

Revelation 2:2-5 {AMP}

In verses 2 & 3 we see an example of what looks like the *Perfect Christian*; someone that is courageous, persistent, and hard working; someone who does not grow weary of doing good, cannot stand evil and even has the ability to weed out apostolic pretenders. But then verses 4 & 5 immediately put a dampener on all the good works. Here we see that all the good work could well be in vain if God Himself is not number one on our priority list.

---

*...what these special individuals shared with The Almighty is purely a shadow of the depth of relationship we can have with our Father*

---

From the time God made man He had relationship on His mind, and I guess that explains why it does not bring joy to His heart when we choose not to spend quality time with Him. The truth is no job, no riches, no relationship, and no Godly service can take the place of a one to one, face to face relationship with God. If they do then they have become idols.

After taking a brief look at the lives of Abraham, Isaac, Jacob, Moses and David we realise that the reason why their portraits are mounted on the walls of Faith's Hall of Fame is simply because they shared something special with God. The relationship they had with God was built on the foundation of faith; a necessary prerequisite when it comes to pleasing God *{Hebrew 11:6}*. However, though enviable, what these special individuals shared with The Almighty is purely a shadow of the depth of relationship we can have with our Father. In Christ we are saved by grace through faith. In Christ we are reconciled to our Father. In Christ we are complete and made whole! If we can actually come to understand who we are in Christ, and walk in the light of this truth, I believe that our walk with our Father will definitely become a lot more exciting.

Well, that is all from me but before I go here are a few words that were dropped in my heart awhile back. I pray they will continually remind you of God's ever-present presence and just how precious you are in His sight:

*Maybe you don't realise*
*You're the apple of My eye*
*Your name is engraved on the palm of My hand*
*You are the reason I died*
*I love you with a love that's so deep*
*Goes beyond what any eye can see*
*And though you may not see Me physically*
*My presence with you is so real*

*When you're hurting inside*
*Makes Me want to cry*
*A feeling so hard to deny*

*No matter what you're going through*
*I will always be there for you*
*Call on Me*
*I'm right here*
*I'll hold your hand*
*I'll hear your prayer*
*Call on Me*
*It doesn't matter what you're going through*
*I'm here and I'm waiting for you*

# DEAR HEAVENLY FATHER,...

Having read this book I enter into a life time journey of
seeking You.
Today I ask for a hunger and a thirst that will no longer
be satisfied by just knowing about You,
A hunger and a thirst that can only be satisfied
by knowing You for myself.

I know You long for a face to face relationship with me
And the response of my heart today is YES!
**I say yes to my Creator,**
who created me to have intimate fellowship with Him;
**I say yes to my Redeemer,**
who chooses to express His manifold wisdom
through me;
**I say yes to my Father,**
who truly loves me unconditionally.

Father, I desire to know You for myself,
Please draw me close to You.
In Jesus name,
Amen